HEROES OF HISTORY

FREDERICK DOUGLASS

The Right to Dignity

HEROES OF HISTORY

FREDERICK DOUGLASS

The Right to Dignity

JANET & GEOFF BENGE

Emerald Books

P.O. BOX 635, LYNNWOOD, WA 98046

Frederick Douglass: The Right to Dignity

Published by Emerald Books
P.O. Box 635
Lynnwood, WA 98046

www.Heroesofhistory.com

Cataloging-in-Publication Data is on file at the Library of Congress.

ISBN 978-1-62486-151-2

First printing 2022

Printed in the United States of America

HEROES OF HISTORY

Abraham Lincoln
Alan Shepard
Ben Carson
Benjamin Franklin
Benjamin Rush
Billy Graham
Captain John Smith
Christopher Columbus
Clara Barton
Davy Crockett
Daniel Boone
Douglas MacArthur
Dwight Eisenhower
Elizabeth Fry
Ernest Shackleton
Frederick Douglass
George Washington
George Washington Carver
Harriet Tubman
John Adams
Laura Ingalls Wilder
Louis Zamperini
Meriwether Lewis
Milton Hershey
Orville Wright
Ronald Reagan
Theodore Roosevelt
Thomas Edison
William Bradford
William Penn
William Wilberforce

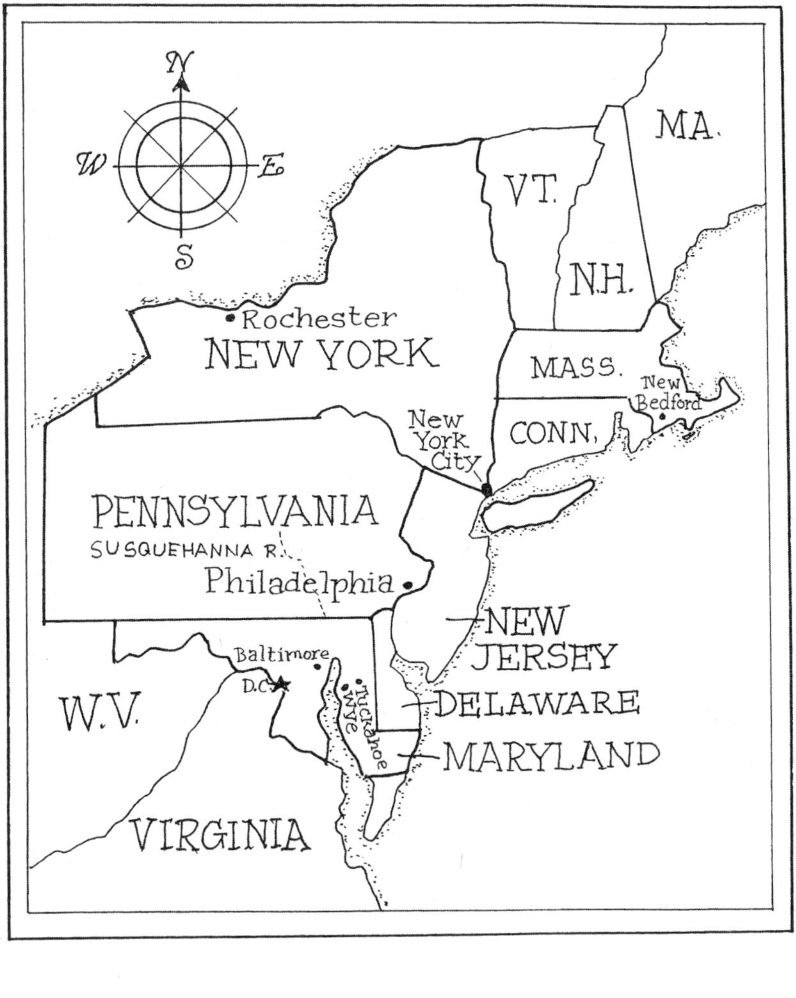
N
W
E
S
MA.
VT.
N.H.
Rochester
NEW YORK
MASS.
New Bedford
New York City
CONN.
PENNSYLVANIA
SUSQUEHANNA R.
Philadelphia
NEW JERSEY
Baltimore
D.C.
Tuckahoe
Wye
DELAWARE
W.V.
MARYLAND
VIRGINIA

Contents

Chapter 1

The Entrance to a Long, Dark Tunnel

Today was different. Frederick could feel it in the air. Grandma Betsy threw an extra corncake on the skillet for him, and Grandpa Isaac lingered a little longer before hitching an axe over his shoulder and heading out to cut firewood. After Isaac left the cabin, Grandma Betsy said, "This mornin' it's time for a long walk. Better say goodbye to everyone." Frederick looked around at the gaggle of children living in his grandparents' cabin with him. There were several cousins and his little sisters Kitty and Arianna, the youngest, who was just starting to talk.

Frederick felt a knot grow in his stomach. It felt like he was standing in the sunlight at the entrance to a long, dark tunnel. Although only six years old, Frederick knew that he had an older brother, Perry, and two older sisters, Sarah and Eliza. They had entered the tunnel before him, along with his cousins Tom, Betsy, Henny, and Nancy. They had all once lived with his grandparents in the same one-room cabin at Holme Hill Farm. They were all long gone—so long gone, Frederick couldn't remember any of them. Now it was his turn to leave behind the cabin and Tuckahoe Creek and the huge walnut tree under which he played while Grandma Betsy sat for hours knotting together seine nets to sell.

Sensing that things would never again be the same, Frederick scanned the inside of the log cabin where he'd been born and lived his whole life. He remembered the first time his grandmother let him climb the ladder to the loft to sleep in the hay. He saw the hole dug into the clay floor in front of the fireplace where Grandma Betsy stored sweet potatoes during the long, cold winters. Frederick knew she was something of a legend on Maryland's Eastern Shore for her ability to know when and how deep to plant sweet potatoes for the best crop.

Frederick watched his grandmother adjust the red bandana tied around her hair. "Ain't no use dawdling. Time to go," she said, stepping out of the windowless cabin. With a final look behind him, Frederick fell into step beside Grandma Betsy as they set out past the well. He noticed the bucket resting on the fork of a tree and the old tobacco shed where he and his cousins often sheltered from the rain. His coarse linen tunic, the only clothing he'd ever worn, flapped against his legs. His hands were empty.

They kicked up dust as they walked westward. The path led across the cornfield to Tapper's Corner and then on to Thimbletown, where they turned slightly north into a stretch of thick forest called Lloyd's Long Woods.

"Lots of things called Lloyd's round here. That's on account of the Lloyd family being here for over a hundred years and owning just about everything in sight," Grandma Betsy explained, glancing down at Frederick. "Don't forget your kin's been here as long as the Lloyds—twisted together as those branches overhead."

Frederick looked up at the tangle of branches. He sensed his grandmother was telling him something important, but it was hard for him to grasp. He'd heard of Governor Lloyd but never seen him in real life. The only thing he knew about the Lloyds and their "Great House" was that many members of his family, including his older siblings and cousins, had all walked this same path from Grandma Betsy's cabin through the countryside to the Great House at the Wye Plantation. From there his family had never returned. Frederick shuddered at the thought. He held his grandmother's hand tightly as the path wound into a dense forest.

Walking among the trees, Frederick's imagination played tricks. He saw monsters with sharp teeth and leering eyes in the tree trunks and ghosts bobbing in the branches. It was all he could do to keep walking along the unknown path.

When they emerged from the woods, the sun was overhead, and Frederick no longer needed to squint.

He and Grandma Betsy continued west, and after a while sat down beside a stream to share a corncake and some water. When it was time to move on, Frederick's legs were wobbly. "I guess twelve miles is a good hike for a little 'un," Grandma Betsy said, reaching down and hoisting Frederick onto her shoulders like a sack of firewood.

Frederick had never been carried this way, mainly, he realized, because he'd never walked this far before. Until today the farthest he'd been from his grandparents' cabin was the short walk to Levi Lee's mill, where he'd spent many hours watching farmers drive wagons filled with corn up to the mill to be ground into meal. Frederick wondered if he would ever again sit by the pond and watch the laden wagons and busy mill.

After being carried for half a mile or so, Frederick was ready to walk again. The land around was changing from forest to more orderly fields filled with rows of wheat. The smell wafting on the breeze was also changing. A hint of herring stew, which Frederick loved to eat, permeated the air.

"We nearly there," Grandma Betsy said. "I ain't got much to tell you 'cept keep your mouth shut and your eyes open. Do everything you're told, and do it mighty quick. You got that?"

Frederick felt a lump in his throat. He nodded, afraid of what his grandmother wasn't telling him. Grandma Betsy stopped and grabbed Frederick by his shoulders. "Frederick Augustus Washington Bailey, you just remember who you are." Frederick nodded. He didn't want to disobey his grandmother, but he had no idea what she meant.

"This here's the Long Green Lane. We'll soon be there," Grandma Betsy announced.

In the distance Frederick made out sounds he hadn't heard before. There was banging and clanging as they walked past an open shed where a man pounded red-hot metal on an anvil. The man looked up briefly and nodded at Grandma Betsy. As they passed another simple building, Frederick caught a glimpse of one man sawing a long plank, while beyond him in the dark recesses of the shed another man hammered.

The Long Green Lane led Frederick through an expanse that rolled gently down toward the water's edge, where a wooden dock was located. "That there's the Wye River," his grandmother told him as she gestured. "And this here Long Green Lane is the center of the Wye Plantation."

To their left they passed low brick buildings around which people gathered. Through the trees Frederick caught a glimpse of a white mansion with six red brick chimneys. "That's the Great Farmhouse," Grandma Betsy told him. "We goin' over yonder to visit Aunt Katy."

Frederick and Grandma Betsy walked on a few more yards until they came to a square white house. Several children played around its entrance. "Grandmammy!" Frederick heard one of the children exclaim as they approached the house. His grandmother turned and smiled. "Now, Frederick, you go on and play. They're your kin. That's your brother,

Perry, and you've got two sisters, Sarah and Eliza, here somewhere." She gave him a gentle nudge. "Go get yourself acquainted."

While reluctant to let go of Grandma Betsy's hand, Frederick wanted to look like a big boy. He slowly edged his way toward the other children.

"You know how to play knucklebones?" a girl asked.

Frederick shook his head. He knew how to play, but right now he didn't feel like it. Instead, he stood with his back to a wall and watched. About seven or eight children, all different shades of black or brown and all different ages, were staring at him. Suddenly a voice broke into Frederick's thoughts. "Frederick, Frederick, Grandmammy's gone!"

The dull ache in Frederick's stomach turned to a sharp pain as he rushed to the door. A large woman stood with her back to him. It wasn't Grandma Betsy. Despite his effort to appear brave, Frederick burst into tears—tears of anger, tears of betrayal, tears of pure terror.

Frederick's ten-year-old brother, Perry, walked over to him holding a peach. "Here," he said, "eat this. It'll make you feel better." Without thinking, or even knowing what it was, Frederick grabbed the peach from his brother's hand and hurled it to the ground. Deep inside he knew his life had taken a drastic and irreversible turn for the worse, and he would not accept anything to soothe that fact.

It took Frederick several days to sort out who he was with and what was expected of him. He was now living on the Wye Plantation, where life revolved around the Great Farmhouse and its owner, Edward Lloyd. The governor, as he was known, was a member of the fifth generation of Lloyds to live on the property. In his mid-forties, Edward Lloyd had already served as the governor of Maryland and was now a United States senator. He'd been born into both wealth and high political standing. Each generation of Lloyds had acquired more land and more slaves to work it until the place was now like a private village. The Lloyd family owned the land as far as Frederick could see in every direction. Their vast landholdings were divided into twelve farms, each with its own set of slaves, its own overseer, and its own set of record-keeping books. Each farm overseer was charged with making as much profit as possible from the land he oversaw while spending as little as possible on caring for the slaves who worked it.

When the governor was away from Wye Plantation on political business, he left Captain Aaron Anthony in charge of his affairs. Grandma Betsy referred to him as "Ol' Master." Along with his daughter, Miss Lucretia, and her new husband, Captain Thomas Auld, Captain Anthony lived in the square white house Frederick's grandmother had taken him to. At the back of the house stood the kitchen, over which Aunt Katy presided.

Frederick counted fourteen people living and working in and around Captain Anthony's house and kitchen. Much to his surprise, he learned they were all his relatives. Along with Aunt Katy, who was his mother's cousin, and Katy's four children, there were Frederick's mother's two younger sisters,

Hester and Milly; Milly's four children; Frederick's older brother, Perry; and his two older sisters, Sarah and Eliza. Frederick was even more surprised to learn that as slaves, none of them belonged to Governor Lloyd. Instead, they were all—including Grandma Betsy back at Holme Hill Farm—owned by Captain Aaron Anthony.

One of Frederick's first jobs at Wye Plantation was driving the dairy cows in for milking twice a day. Frederick was also responsible for keeping the chickens out of the kitchen garden and raking the leaves from the yard and paths around Captain Anthony's house. The work was simple, and Frederick enjoyed outsmarting the chickens.

As the newest member of the Anthony household, Frederick learned he had to compete for whatever food he could get to eat. Although Captain Anthony had arranged for all fourteen of his slaves to get three meals a day—thick slabs of cornbread for breakfast and dinner and slop for lunch—Aunt Katy had determined that her three sons should get most of the food, often letting the others go hungry. The noon meal was the only one Frederick could count on. It consisted mostly of cornmeal mush that Aunt Katy poured into the wooden trough she placed on the kitchen floor or outside. Once the trough was filled, the children were called and came running to fight over its contents. With oyster shells, pieces of bark, or old roof shingles, they scooped out the cornmeal mush. Frederick learned he had to eat fast to get enough food and that the strongest children were able to muscle themselves into the best position at the trough. He was neither strong nor practiced at scooping up cornmeal mush with an oyster shell. He often went hungry, so hungry that he took to eating the kitchen scraps meant for Old Nep, the dog. When Old Nep beat him to the scraps, Frederick didn't eat.

As the newcomer at the Anthony home, Frederick had to sleep wherever he could find a place. He settled on a cupboard in the kitchen. Adult slaves were given a blanket, but children had to find their own source of warmth at night. Frederick used a cornmeal sack in which he slept headfirst on the cupboard's dirt floor, his feet dangling from the sack's opening.

As summer faded into fall, Frederick often felt cold as well as hungry. The only things he owned were two linen tunics, each one worn for a week at a time and then washed. The tunics came to his knees, but he had no shoes or pants to keep his feet and legs warm. He learned to stay on the sunny side of the kitchen, especially against the wooden walls, which reflected some warmth. Despite this, large cracks opened between his toes that bled on especially cold days.

Aunt Katy arose at dawn and would pound on the cupboard door to wake Frederick. His first job each day was to fetch water from the well. Sometimes Aunt Katy asked him to run errands for her, which Frederick looked forward to. Using the errands as an excuse, he began exploring the contained world of the Wye Plantation. He discovered that about 150 slaves were working there. He was fascinated with everything about the place, from the horses to the pigs, sheep, cows, ducks, and chickens. And there were many buildings, each with its own purpose. There were stables where the horses were kept, the carpenter's workshop, the blacksmith's building with its fiery forge, and the creamery where cows' milk was churned into butter or made into cheese. Then there was the smokehouse where hams and slabs of bacon were cured and smoked.

Frederick learned that Governor Lloyd loved sports that involved animals—dead or alive—horse racing, cockfighting, and deer hunting on his own deer park. The governor also bred Newfoundland dogs and owned a champion racehorse, which Old Barney and his son, Young Barney, took care of. Under their oversight the Lloyd stable was considered the best in Maryland.

Wherever Frederick went, curiosity helped him make friends, including Miss Lucretia, Captain Anthony's twenty-one-year-old married daughter. She became someone he learned to rely upon. He discovered that if he stood outside her window and sang, Miss Lucretia would smile and often give him a piece of bread and butter to eat. And when Frederick was hit on the head with a stone at the blacksmith's workshop, Aunt Katy just scolded him, while Miss Lucretia took him into her parlor and bathed and bandaged his wound.

Governor Lloyd owned everything for as far as Frederick could see or imagine, but he was also an aloof figure. He was often away from the plantation socializing or taking care of political business in Baltimore or Washington, D.C. As a result, Frederick was surprised to learn that Governor Lloyd had noticed him. Captain Anthony delivered the news that the governor wanted a companion and servant for his youngest son, twelve-year-old Daniel, and had chosen Frederick for the job. Frederick wondered what this change might mean for him.

Chapter 2

Two Entirely Different Worlds

Despite his new position, Frederick learned that he was still under the watchful eye of Aunt Katy. He had to do her bidding each morning, while Daniel Lloyd and his sisters Ann and Mary were tutored. During the afternoons, however, Frederick served as Daniel's companion. Of course, he had strict rules to follow. Frederick was an outdoor companion and not permitted to set foot inside the Lloyd mansion. Although Daniel was six years older than Frederick, the two boys quickly learned to trust each other. They hunted rabbits, visited the windmill near Long Point, and roamed the banks of the Wye River estuary, stopping sometimes to swim in the shallow bays. As they swam or walked along the estuary, sometimes they saw coastal sailing vessels plying the estuary. Frederick loved watching them.

Daniel explained that just a few miles to the west, bigger, more magnificent sailing ships were headed down Chesapeake Bay from Baltimore and Annapolis bound for other ports across the Atlantic Ocean in England and Europe.

During their afternoon adventures, Daniel fired Frederick's imagination with tales of what went on inside the Great Farmhouse and the equally magnificent Orangery greenhouse located behind it. During summer all sorts of people visited and stayed at the house. Many, including Daniel's uncle, Francis Scott Key, held high positions in government. According to Daniel, more people passed through the Great Farmhouse than stayed at nearby Easton Hotel, which his father also owned.

Frederick didn't ask too many questions, but little by little he gained ideas and impressions about the outside world. When Daniel told him that the first Lloyd family mansion was looted by pirates and burned down by British troops during the Revolutionary War, Frederick struggled to understand the idea of colonies and foreign rulers. But as he continued listening to Daniel, he began piecing together snippets of American history, including the fact that twenty-four states made up the United States and that Canada to the north was still controlled by Great Britain. To the west lay unorganized and Mexican territories.

Although Frederick was only six years old, it was clear to him that a large gap existed between what a slave boy like him knew and Daniel's knowledge. It was as if they inhabited two entirely different worlds.

Frederick longed to know more about Daniel's world and knew that bridging the gap would mean learning to read.

Before long Frederick found himself in a classroom of sorts run by "Uncle" Isaac Copper. Sixty-year-old Isaac was once the slave in charge of breeding fighting cocks for Governor Lloyd. Now he was crippled and instead presided over a school teaching young slaves on the Wye Plantation how to take care of their spiritual and medical needs, as well as teaching them how to read and write. The school, which lasted for an hour each morning, was specifically for Lloyd slaves, though Captain Anthony was allowed to send along his young slaves as well.

Frederick was excited on the first day as he walked into the makeshift schoolhouse. Isaac Copper sat hunched on a three-legged stool at the front of the schoolroom. Frederick soon learned that behind the teacher's welcoming smile resided a mean-spirited old man. Isaac had a selection of willow switches in varying lengths arrayed beside him, such that he could grab one that would let him reach every student in the class, even those at the back of the room. And he didn't hold back using them. For their first lesson he began reciting the Lord's prayer and had the students repeat the words aloud. If a student failed to do so with the right diction or lacked necessary enthusiasm or sincerity, Isaac would take a willow switch and beat him or her mercilessly while never getting up from his stool.

After two days of school, Frederick was done. He'd come to learn to read but so far he hadn't had a single reading lesson. Instead, lessons revolved around reciting prayers and Bible passages while being lashed by Isaac in what the students referred to as Prayin' and Floggin'. On the third day of school Frederick made up an excuse, then another, and another. No one seemed to notice or care that he wasn't at school anymore. His learning to read would have to wait.

Frederick learned that Uncle Isaac wasn't the only person who went about whipping people. As he lay asleep on the dirt floor of the kitchen cupboard one night, the sound of pleading and sobbing seeped into his ears. Frederick untangled himself from his sleeping sack and crawled to the cupboard door. He peered through the cracks between the boards. Chills ran down his spine. His mother's fifteen-year-old sister, Aunt Hester, stood on a bench beside the table. Frederick could make out the silhouette of Captain Anthony, Ol' Master, his back toward the cupboard door. Captain Anthony raised a blue rod, much like the switches Isaac Copper used on students, and brought it down across his aunt's back.

For a moment Frederick looked away in shock. Slowly Aunt Hester's shrieks faded to a whimper as Captain Anthony finished the beating. Then Ol' Master stood up and led Aunt Hester from the kitchen. Frederick huddled in his cupboard shaking in the silence. What had he just witnessed? Why was his aunt beaten so harshly? And by Captain Anthony? What was going to happen to her now? Since coming to the Wye Plantation he'd thought of Ol' Master as being both stern and kind. He never imagined the man could do something like this.

Frederick was glad when morning came. Aunt Katy ordered his sister Sarah to clean up the encrusted pool of blood under the table. Sarah lowered her eyes and set to work with a rag and bowl of water. No one asked where the blood came from or to whom it belonged. Frederick remembered Grandma Betsy's words: "Keep your eyes open and your mouth shut." It seemed like the others had heard the same advice before him.

Later in the day Frederick got up the courage to ask Tom, his eleven-year-old cousin, about the beating he'd witnessed. Tom seemed worldly to Frederick. He was cabin boy on the *Sally Lloyd,* the plantation's sloop that Thomas Auld captained. As cabin boy, Tom had been to Baltimore and Annapolis many times and told wonderful stories of enormous buildings higher than pine trees and church bells that rang loud enough to be heard from the docks. Frederick felt confident that if anyone could help him understand why Aunt Hester had been beaten, it would be Tom.

Instead of answering Frederick's question, Tom told him a story about a slave named Bill Denby, who lived on the Davis Farm, one of the many farms Governor Lloyd owned. A year before Frederick arrived at Wye Plantation, Bill Denby, a strong young man, was being whipped by his overseer, Master Gore. In the middle of the whipping, Bill broke free and plunged into a nearby creek. He made it to the middle, where he stood neck deep in the water. Master Gore demanded he get out of the creek so he could resume the beating, but Bill wouldn't budge. After yelling at him some more, the overseer pulled out a gun and shot Bill, killing him instantly.

According to Tom, the rumor was that Governor Lloyd was angry with Master Gore for killing a valuable piece of the governor's property. A healthy, young male slave such as Bill Denby was valued at four hundred dollars. As far as Tom could tell, the killing was murder, plain and simple. But as he explained to Frederick, in the United States, if a white man was accused of murdering a black man, whether he was a slave or not, it required the witness of a white person to take the matter to court. Since only Master Gore and other slaves had witnessed the shooting, the killing was deemed "necessary" and nothing more was said about it. "Best not to ask why someone is beaten or punished," Tom concluded. "No good can come of it for you or them."

After his conversation with Tom, Frederick tried to understand more about the slaves working in the fields. As he went about Wye Plantation, he watched the Lloyd field slaves closely. He noticed how hard they labored from sunrise to sunset, six days a week. In the evenings they cooked and did their washing and mending. As they walked to the fields each morning, an overseer on horseback watched over them. If a slave was too slow, the overseer would whip him or her with a willow switch, just as Isaac Copper did to students in school. The slaves carried ashcakes with them, which they had cooked in the fire the night before. Frederick noticed how they sang as they worked, even when the work was backbreaking and the summer heat oppressive. He also noticed the ever-present whippings and beatings meted out to slaves who were too slow or sloppy in their work.

When he had the opportunity, Frederick tried to ask the slaves questions, but found their language strange. Most of the slaves on the plantation had lived in the United States for only one or two generations and spoke with a mix of native African languages and heavily accented English. Frederick's family had lived on Maryland's Eastern Shore for at least a hundred years and used few native African words. Frederick was intrigued by the way the field slaves spoke. He realized that the words you used and how clearly you said them made people either pay attention or ignore you. He began wondering how it might feel to use his voice in a different way. He started listening closely to how Daniel pronounced words and would mimic him. Daniel did the same with Frederick's distinctive speech. Soon it became a game to see who sounded more like the other.

One afternoon Frederick and Daniel wandered into the Lloyd family burial ground and sat side by side on a stone seat. Frederick was nervous. Aunt Katy had warned him to avoid the place. She said older slaves had seen ghosts in shrouds riding huge black horses over the graves, while others had spoken of balls of fire flying by at midnight accompanied by unearthly screams. Sitting beside Daniel, Frederick listened as Daniel pointed to the grave of his grandfather, Edward Lloyd IV, who had served in the Continental Congress and personally knew George Washington. There was even a grave for Daniel's great-great-grandfather, Philemon Lloyd, whose father, the first Edward Lloyd, was a Puritan who had come to the American colonies from Wales in the 1600s. He had helped to negotiate a treaty with the Susquehannock tribe for the surrender of territory on the eastern shore of Chesapeake Bay, which became the plantation Frederick now lived on. Daniel also pointed out more recent graves, including that of Elizabeth Lloyd, Daniel's sister who had died as a baby.

All the talk about Lloyd family history unsettled Frederick. Where were the graves of *his* family? What did he know about them compared to Daniel's knowledge of his family? It was difficult for Frederick to think about his father. The other children Aunt Katy ruled over knew who their fathers were, but Frederick didn't know his. He'd been told that his father was a white man, since he was much lighter in color than his mother or grandparents. That made sense to Frederick who, though he had the same tightly curled hair, looked much lighter than the field hands. Frederick had heard a rumor that Aaron Anthony was his father but didn't know if that was fact or fancy. He certainly hoped to find out one day and promised himself he would ask his mother, Harriet Bailey, soon.

Frederick loved it when his mother came to visit him and his siblings at Aunt Katy's kitchen, though her visits were few and far between. He understood why. She had to walk twelve miles to see him and twelve miles back. And since she had no days off from work, she began her journey to see Frederick and his siblings after dark and walked back ready for work at sunup the following morning. She never got to see her children during daylight, but Frederick was glad when she came, even if she was tired and weary and it was late in the day.

Late one evening in February 1825, the kitchen door swung open and in walked his mother. Frederick ran and clung to her as she took a seat on a stool beside the fireplace to warm herself. His eyes grew big when he saw what she had brought for him—a heart-shaped ginger cake. She told Frederick he was her Valentine and hugged him close until he fell asleep in her arms. When he awoke at dawn, Frederick was lying on the floor, the cake beside him and his mother gone. He was sad she'd left, but knew she had to be back to work in the fields at sunup. He broke off a piece of ginger cake and ate it slowly, reliving the feeling of resting in his mother's arms.

Not long after his mother's visit in February, Frederick witnessed Governor Lloyd whip Old Barney. He watched the governor order Old Barney to remove his shirt and kneel on the dusty ground in front of the stable. Head bowed, Old Barney obeyed. Governor Lloyd stepped back to get a good swing and lashed Old Barney's back with a horse whip. When it was over, he stood, bowed slightly to the governor, and stumbled off to wash and bandage his bleeding back.

The sight of bloodied Old Barney walking away depressed Frederick. Old Barney took great pride in grooming and doctoring Governor Lloyd's prize horses and running the stable, which people agreed was the best in the district. Despite all he did, Old

Barney wasn't above being whipped mercilessly by his master. Frederick tried hard not to think about his own future after that. He was currently the favored companion of an important young man on the Wye Plantation. But how long would that last? Would Daniel be sent off to boarding school soon like his oldest brothers? Would he grow tired of Frederick and request another slave boy to accompany him on his daily adventures? What would happen then? The best Frederick could hope for was to work inside the Great Farmhouse, where slaves appeared to have enough food to eat and the master made sure they always looked well-groomed and had warm clothes. Before witnessing the beating, Frederick had wondered if he might one day be allowed to work alongside Old Barney and care for the horses. Now he wanted no part of that.

In late August 1825, Frederick received two pieces of news that made him even more despondent. The first was the news that his mother had died. Aunt Katy told him she'd been sick for several weeks before succumbing. Frederick had known nothing of this. By the time he learned of it, his mother was dead and buried in an unmarked grave. Frederick barely knew what to think about it.

The second piece of news had to do with Aunt Jenny, his mother's sister. She and Uncle Noah, Aunt Katy's brother, were gone—disappeared. Frederick's cousin Tom explained what had probably happened. "They made a run for the north," he said.

"Why would they head north?" Frederick asked.

"They want to be free."

"Free? You mean slaves are free up north?" Frederick asked.

"Sure. If you can get there through all the slave catchers, you got a chance at being free. Ain't no one allowed to keep a slave up north," Tom replied.

Frederick opened his mouth to ask more questions, then quickly shut it. He needed to give this whole idea of freedom some consideration.

That night, lying on the dirt floor in the kitchen cupboard, Frederick tried to come to grips with what he knew about slaves and free people. He knew that his grandfather Isaac, who was black, was a free man. This meant that he could earn his own money felling trees and dressing lumber. But his wife—Grandma Betsy—was a slave, as were all her children. Why was that? What made one person a slave and another free? Now it seemed that if a slave could escape from his or her master and head north, he or she would be free there. Did this mean that some places in the United States had laws against slavery while others didn't? Frederick was astonished. On the one hand it made no sense to him at all. On the other, it offered hope. Frederick promised himself that if Aunt Jenny and Uncle Noah could embark on a journey to find freedom, one day he would too.

This liberating thought was soon tempered by a different reality. Aunt Jenny and Uncle Noah had two children, Mary and Isaac, Frederick's cousins, both around his age. They, too, had lived with Grandma Betsy at Holme Hill Farm. But within a week of being told that his aunt and uncle had made a run for freedom, Frederick learned that Mary and Isaac had been sold to a slave dealer. Two other relatives, his mother's sister, nineteen-year-old Maryann, and his fourteen-year-old cousin Betsy, were also sold with them. Word was they were bound for a cotton plantation in Alabama. In one drop of an auctioneer's gavel, the thin sliver of chord that bound Frederick to four of his family members had been cut.

"They're makin' an example of them," Tom told Frederick, a glum look on his face. "If your kin run away, you get packed south."

Although a 150-dollar reward for the return of Jenny and Noah was advertised in the *Republican Star* newspaper, they were not returned. Frederick was glad, both because that meant they probably made it to freedom and because he couldn't imagine how sad they would be to learn their children were all sold and gone.

As 1825 rolled into 1826, Frederick, who was now eight years old, became even more aware of his precarious situation. In early 1826, Captain Aaron Anthony's health failed, and he was forced to retire and hand over his position as overseer at the Wye Plantation to a younger man. This meant that he, along with all his slaves, would have to move off the plantation. In rapid succession Aunt Katy was hired out to another plantation, and the rest of the kitchen workers and children were taken back to Holme Hill Farm, except for Frederick. His stomach churned as he awaited his fate.

Chapter 3

City Boy

Sheep bleated and pressed against Frederick's new woolen trousers as he stood on the aft deck of the *Sally Lloyd*. He could barely believe his luck. Three days before, Lucretia Auld had told him he was being sent to Baltimore as a companion for Tommy, her nephew. Tommy's father, Hugh, was the younger brother of Thomas Auld, Miss Lucretia's husband. Frederick imagined Tommy to be about the same age as Daniel Lloyd until Miss Lucretia's told him Tommy was a two-year-old.

"Trim the foresail," the helmsman yelled. Frederick grinned as he watched his cousin Tom and other sailors spring into action. How many times had Tom described what it was like being on a sailing sloop? He'd talked about the rocking and rolling motion of the vessel and the exhilaration of wind filling the billowing sails. Now Frederick was experiencing these things himself.

The *Sally Lloyd* moved out into Eastern Bay, and Frederick took one last look back at the Wye River estuary before he pushed past the sheep and stepped over the rope penning them on the aft deck. He made his way to the foredeck and sat down on a stack of canvas covers near the bow. It felt too good to be true. Finally—unexpectedly—he was leaving behind Captain Anthony and Governor Lloyd and all the misery he'd endured under Aunt Katy's authority.

Of course, Frederick knew he wouldn't really be free. Captain Anthony still owned him. He was just on loan to the Auld family. Mrs. Auld would soon be giving birth to another child, and someone was needed to watch her two-year-old. Frederick imagined what living with a family in a house in the city would be like. Would he sleep inside with them or in a shed behind the house? Would they make him stay inside all day, or would he be able to take Tommy for walks? Would Mrs. Auld be kind like Miss Lucretia, or would she always have the whip handy? Questions washed over Frederick like the foamy waves bursting against the bow of the *Sally Lloyd.*

As the hours passed, the sloop sailed down Eastern Bay, rounded Kent Point, and headed into the main channel of Chesapeake Bay. Around them were other boats—fishing boats and large ships with sails unfurled. Tom told Frederick that the boats around them were approaching the narrowest point on Chesapeake Bay. The *Sally Lloyd* headed north for a distance, then tacked west. As they got closer to land, Frederick could see columns of smoke rising from factory chimneys and small houses hugging the shoreline. Then, Annapolis, Maryland's capital, came into view where the *Sally Lloyd* docked at the mouth of the Severn River. Two gentlemen who had been visiting the Wye Plantation disembarked. Frederick remembered Daniel telling him about the Lloyds' three-story red brick home in Annapolis, but he had no time to go and see it. As soon as the two men disembarked, the *Sally Lloyd* cast off, hoisted her sails, and headed back out into Chesapeake Bay.

When night fell, Frederick bedded down beside Tom on the lower deck. He lay on a pile of straw listening to the hull timbers creak and groan while the sheep bleated on the deck above. Frederick was too excited to sleep.

At sunup the next day—Sunday—Frederick was on deck scanning the shoreline as the *Sally Lloyd* sailed into Baltimore harbor and prepared to dock. He'd thought Annapolis large and busy, but Baltimore was huge. Tom had told him it was the third largest city in the United States, but Frederick hadn't grasped what that really meant until now. Ships sat at anchor in the harbor while others were tied up alongside the quays lining the inner harbor. From the harbor's edge, houses and other buildings fanned out as far as Frederick could see. To the northwest they stretched up the side of a hill onto a plateau that divided Baltimore into a lower and an upper city. Smoke billowed from chimneys while church bells rang across the city.

The *Sally Lloyd* docked at Smith's Wharf. Frederick was immediately aware of the noise and activity going on all around. Barrels of molasses and rum from the West Indies were being offloaded from some ships docked at the wharf, as were sacks of guano from Peru and Brazilian coffee from other countries, while wheat and oats destined for Europe were being put aboard other ships. Dogs barked and sailors yelled back and forth to each other, but it seemed to Frederick that the slaves, stripped to the waist, their bodies glistening with sweat, were doing the heavy work.

With the *Sally Lloyd* tied up alongside the wharf, Frederick was assigned to help guide the sheep through Baltimore's cobblestoned streets to the Curtis slaughterhouse. The homes lining the streets intrigued him. They were joined together in rows, the sidewall of one marking the beginning of the next house. Scrubbed brick steps led up to front doors adorned with shiny brass knockers. Frederick was also amazed by how busy the streets were. At the Wye Plantation Frederick had only ever seen a few people at a time visiting the Lloyd's Great Farmhouse. But Baltimore was abuzz with white people making their way to church as they bowed and nodded to one another. The men wore fine clothes and felt hats, and the women wore wide, hooped dresses. Some people walked. Others rode in carriages. Many black people were also on the streets. They seemed to walk purposefully. Some talked and laughed among themselves and held their heads high.

After driving the sheep to the slaughterhouse, Frederick made his way back to Smith's Wharf.

Once aboard the *Sally Lloyd,* the captain ordered Wilson, one of the free sailors, to escort Frederick to the Aulds' house. Unlike the rich men who had disembarked in Annapolis the day before with various boxes and bags, Frederick had nothing to carry. He wore everything he owned. As they walked down the gangplank, the captain yelled after Wilson, "Make it fast. There's more unloading to be done here."

Once more Frederick's senses were flooded with unfamiliar sights and sounds as he and Wilson made their way through Fells Point, a labyrinth of winding streets and alleys. Before long Frederick was climbing the front steps to a dilapidated two-story house on Aliceanna Street. The door opened, and there stood three figures, a man who looked like a shorter version of Thomas Auld and a woman in a green plaid dress with a toddler peeking out shyly from behind her.

"Here's Frederick. The captain sends his greetings. I'll be off now," Wilson announced. Turning to Frederick and before pressing his hand on Frederick's back and propelling him across the threshold of the door, he added, "Do as you're told if you want to stay here."

The woman took Frederick's hand and smiled. "So, you are here at last! You can call me Miss Sophia, and this is Tommy." The toddler looked up at Frederick with a frown. "Your main job is to take care of him," Miss Sophia said.

Frederick nodded, "Yes, ma'am, I'll do my best." He spoke in the same tone of voice Daniel Lloyd used. Miss Sophia raised her eyebrows and looked at her husband, Hugh. "Yes, I think you will do nicely," she said, ushering Frederick inside the house.

As the day progressed, Frederick's mind whirled at the novelty of his new living quarters. Miss Sophia showed him his room—situated in a loft above the kitchen that was all his. There was a bed with a thick layer of straw that had blankets and two quilts on top of it. Beside the bed was a small table like the one Aunt Kate used to rest her feet on in the evenings. The day was filled with many firsts—the first time Frederick had ever sat at a table to eat food, the first time he'd played with a white toddler, and the first time he'd climbed into his own bed.

It took Frederick several weeks to get accustomed to sleeping in the soft bed, eating at a table with a family, and being spoken to kindly throughout the day. It was particularly difficult for him to look a white person in the eye, but Miss Sophia insisted he do so. "Look up," she would remind him when he spoke to her. "Don't be afraid." He also grew to love Tommy, an inquisitive little boy who peppered him with questions.

One of Frederick's daily duties was to collect water from the town pump at the corner of Washington Street. Each morning he took the pail hanging beside the back door and walked west on Aliceanna Street, which ran through the heart of Fells Point. The area was home to many shipbuilding yards where Baltimore's famed clippers, the fastest ships in the world, were constructed. The place was a maze of carpentry shops, sailmaking lofts, warehouses, and pubs packed with sea captains and sailors from places as far afield as South America, Europe, and Africa. Wherever you went in Fells Point, the sound of clanging, banging, thumping, and yelling from the shipyards and docks filled the air.

As he made his way to collect water, Frederick couldn't help noticing the huge sixty-four-gun frigate towering over the Fells Point docks. This was the *Constituicao,* commissioned by the empire of Brazil for its navy and the biggest ship ever built at Fells Point. Hugh Auld was a builder on the project and gave daily accounts at dinner about how far behind schedule construction of the ship was and why.

On May 11, two months after Frederick's arrival in Baltimore, businesses in Fells Point shut down as the community came together to celebrate the launch of the *Constituicao.* It was a day for festivities and picnics. By mid-morning a crowd had gathered by the shipyard where the vessel had been built, and the people jostled one another for the best view. Frederick, holding Tommy's hand tightly, was among the throng. He watched as shipyard workers wielding large hammers knocked away the supports shoring up the ship. When the final support was removed, the *Constituicao* slid backward. It was a majestic sight as the frigate took to the water for the first time, a scene Frederick was sure he'd never forget.

Another amazing thing Frederick observed among the throng of people who gathered was that it was made up of both black and white people, both young and old. They laughed and sang together and cheered and clapped loudly as the *Constituicao* was launched. It was a scene he could never have imagined when he lived on the Wye Plantation. Frederick hoped he would never have to leave Baltimore.

One night, napping under the table in the parlor, Frederick awoke to hear Miss Sophia reading aloud from her Bible. "Wherefore then hast thou brought me forth out of the womb? Oh that I had given up the ghost, and no eye had seen me! I should have been as though I had not been; I should have been carried from the womb to the grave. Are not my days few? cease then, and let me alone, that I may take comfort a little." Something stirred deep inside Frederick as he heard the words being read. Back at the Wye Plantation, when Uncle Isaac Copper tried to teach him to read, Frederick escaped class as soon as he could. Now, hearing such poetic words, even though he couldn't fully understand them, made Frederick yearn to read.

The following morning, after Hugh had left for work, Frederick asked Miss Sophia if she would teach him to read. She agreed, and he started learning his ABCs. He was a quick learner and soon progressed to sounding out simple three-letter words.

Frederick considered how well his life had turned out. He fetched water in the morning to fill the cistern at the back of the house, watched over Tommy, taking him for walks and playing with him, and continued his reading lessons with Miss Sophia.

In November, news reached the Auld family that Frederick's legal owner, Captain Aaron Anthony, had died. Miss Sophia told Frederick that the captain had died without a will. This meant that there would be a long legal process to find out who should inherit his property, including his twenty-nine slaves. Everyone would just have to wait and see what would happen.

It took the court nearly a year to decide how Aaron Anthony's property should be distributed among his three children, Andrew and Richard Anthony and their sister, Lucretia Auld. But before everything was finally settled, Miss Lucretia died in childbirth. Her share of the estate would be passed on to her husband, Thomas Auld.

On a windy day in early October 1827, Frederick found himself standing by the gangplank of the schooner *Wildcat*, on which he was to return across Chesapeake Bay. He'd been summoned back to the Eastern Shore to learn his fate in the division of Aaron Anthony's estate. As he said goodbye to the Auld family, Miss Sophia burst into tears, Tommy howled with anguish, and Tommy's young sister Ann joined in. For his part, Frederick was numb. He'd experienced a big city and known the luxury of living in a house. He had been treated more like a stepson than a slave by Miss Sophia. Most amazingly, he'd seen other black people going about their business free and in charge of themselves. His worst fear was that he might be sold south as Mary and Isaac, Aunt Jenny's children, had been.

Two nights later, Frederick stood outside Grandma Betsy's hut at Holme Hill Farm. The place was much smaller and dingier than he remembered. His grandmother was now in her mid-fifties and bent with age. Many of Frederick's Bailey relatives were already assembled, but others were still arriving from farms and plantations to which they had been hired out. As they gathered, Frederick felt very much different from his relatives. He and his cousin Tom were the only ones who had been across Chesapeake Bay to the Western Shore, and he was the only one who had lived in a white person's house. His vocabulary and way of speaking were different from his aunts, uncles, and cousins. He wore "Big House" clothes and could make his way around a city alone.

The following morning, Aunt Hester pointed out Frederick's mother's grave to him. It was a raised mound of dirt with a few pebbles placed over it. Frederick realized the other mounds nearby must mark the graves of various other relatives. He couldn't help but think of the contrast with the Lloyd family graveyard where he'd spent time with Daniel Lloyd. There each grave was marked with a cross or a monument or a raised brick structure where the name of each of Daniel's ancestors was recorded, along with his or her birth and death date, spanning back over one hundred years. Meanwhile, the Bailey family didn't have a single marker to commemorate their lives.

Over the next few days, Frederick overheard several conversations among the older members of the family. He gleaned from these that being allotted to Andrew Anthony was universally considered to be the worst option. As a young man, Andrew had gone west to Indiana and returned three years later with a wife, Ann, and a serious drinking and gambling habit. All agreed that if they went to Andrew, it wouldn't be long before they were separated from one another and sold south to pay off one of his gambling debts.

On Thursday morning, October 18, Frederick took his place in a lineup along with his four sisters, one brother, eight cousins, and assorted aunts and uncles to learn his fate. Everyone was quiet, even the smallest children seemed to understand the gravity of the situation. Soon some men arrived with pens and paper in hand. They proceeded to walk down the line of Frederick's relatives, every so often stopping to ask a question, inspect someone's teeth, or pinch the skin on the back of the person's hand. The men talked quietly when they came to his cousin Henny, who had badly injured both hands in a fire when she was an infant. Grandma Betsy stood watching at the end of the line. Frederick felt compassion for the old woman whom he admired so much as she watched her five daughters and her son, along with fourteen grandchildren, being appraised like cattle to be divided and scattered far and wide. The Baileys had been a proud Eastern Shore family for many generations. Now, with the flourish of a pen, it would all end.

Once the men reached the end of the line, they called out names and divided the family into three lots, each valued at about $930. Frederick watched as Grandma Betsy was told to stand to the left along with his siblings Perry, now a strong young field hand, and Sarah, Eliza, Kitty, and Arianna. Aunt Betty and Frederick's cousins Stephen and Angela joined them. "You now belong to Andrew Anthony," one of the men announced. Next Aunt Katy, her three sons, and a daughter were set off to the right, along with Aunt Hester, her newborn son, Aunt Prissy, and several others whom Frederick did not recognize. He held his breath, waiting to hear who they would be allotted to. "You all are now the property of Richard Anthony," he heard the man say.

A surge of relief raced through Frederick. His group, which included his older sister, Eliza; Aunt Priscilla; Aunt Milly, and her four children, Tom, Henny, Nancy, and a baby were going to Thomas Auld. Frederick wondered if it was possible that Thomas Auld would send him back to Baltimore.

Chapter 4

Was Reading That Powerful?

Much to his relief, by Christmas 1827, Frederick was back in Baltimore with the Auld family. Miss Sophia and Tommy welcomed him again, and Frederick hoped that everything would be just as it was before. However, a shadow had fallen over them all, and Frederick's heart was heavy with the weight of truly understanding that he was enslaved. He was owned by a white man, and any whim or change of circumstance in that person's life could devastate his own. It seemed to Frederick that the Auld family, especially Hugh Auld, were not as happy to see him back in Baltimore as he'd thought they would be.

One evening, Hugh came home after work smelling of brandy, as he often did lately. Frederick was in the kitchen, reading three-letter words to Miss Sophia as she stirred some soup. "Good evening," she said to her husband. "I'm proud of Frederick. He's quick with his letters. He'll be reading soon."

Hugh turned white. "You mean you're teaching that slave boy to read?"

"Why yes," Miss Sophia said. "One afternoon he listened as I read aloud from the Book of Job and then asked me to teach him how to read. It's hardly taken him any time at all."

"Think what you are doing!" Hugh bellowed. "Learning will spoil the best slave in the world. He needs only enough learning to understand what we want him to do." Hugh paused for a moment to take a breath. "If you teach that boy to read, he'll long for freedom! Illiterate slaves know their place in this world. Do you want him to learn to read and then determine to escape?"

Frederick stood perfectly still. He'd never heard anyone talk about learning to read that way before. Was it true that reading would stir up ideas of freedom? Could reading books, newspapers, and magazines show him a path north—out of slavery? Was reading that powerful?

"Oh," Miss Sophia responded, clapping the book shut. "I'm sorry. I didn't think of it like that. The last thing I want to do is to unsettle Frederick. Have your wish, dear. That will be the last time I instruct the boy."

Frederick's heart dropped at her words. But although he might have just had his last reading lesson from Miss Sophia, he now had a glimpse into the power of reading. He knew for certain he would find a way to teach himself more words.

True to her word, Miss Sophia refused to answer any questions Frederick had about reading. He noticed other subtle changes in the way she treated him. Miss Sophia stopped reading the Bible aloud when Frederick was around and didn't put her arm on his shoulder or offer him words of encouragement as she'd done before. In fact, sometimes in public she spoke harshly to him. Frederick sensed he had lost a friend and ally.

In the weeks following his return, many other changes were taking place in the Auld household. Miss Sophia was expecting another baby, and the family moved several blocks south to a row house on Philpot Street. From the tiny window in his attic room, Frederick could see the docks on the far side of the street. Hugh had gone into partnership with Edward Harrison, and they began building their own ships. Frederick wondered if the stress of the new business had caused the adults around him to become unsettled.

Late in the afternoons, Miss Sophia would allow Frederick to venture outside on his own. He soon made friends with other children living on and around Philpot Street. They were the sons of Irish, Scottish, and German immigrants: Charlie Farity, Gustavus Dorgan, and brothers Jim, Bill, and George Cordery. Although he was black and enslaved, Frederick was daring and good at games, and the local boys at Fells Point quickly accepted him as an equal.

Whenever he could, Frederick practiced reading. Although all around him were words to read on street signs, on the sides of dray carts, and in shop windows, it was frustrating for him not to be able to ask Miss Sophia questions.

After Frederick had been back in Baltimore two years, his life changed yet again. He realized that money must be short for the Auld family because even though there was a new baby, Benjamin Franklin Auld, Hugh Auld insisted it was time for Frederick to work at the Auld and Harrison shipyard. Instead of spending his days with women and children, eleven-year-old Frederick was thrust into the world of working white men.

Frederick soon learned the ins and outs of the jobs assigned him. He had to split wood and stoke the fire under the pitch box and watch over the shipyard when the men went home for lunch. He turned the grindstone every morning so the workers could sharpen their adzes and chisels for the day. And he had to pick oakum. This involved picking through piles of used rope, scraping off the tar used to seal it, and then unraveling the strands of the rope and laying their fibers out in a single direction. The oakum was then used by caulkers to seal the gaps between the planks on the hulls and decks of ships at the shipyard.

Hugh bought old ropes by the hundredweight, and Frederick soon understood why prisoners and disobedient sailors were often forced to pick oakum for weeks on end. The wiry flax fibers embedded themselves into the skin between his fingers, and his hands ached so much at night it was difficult to sleep. Frederick much preferred to run errands for the shipyard, checking on an order of cordage from the ropewalk, fetching brass fittings for a ship's railing, or rolling empty barrels back to the turpentine merchant.

One lunchtime not long after starting work at the shipyard, Frederick had time to ponder the chalked letters carpenters scribbled on the ends of planks of wood to indicate where they were to be used. There was *s* for starboard, *l* for larboard, *sa* for starboard aft, *sf* for starboard forward, *la* for larboard aft, and *lf* for larboard forward.

By now Frederick could read simple sentences but didn't know how to write letters. While the men left the shipyard for lunch, he used the time they were gone to practice writing. He began copying the carpenter's letters on the ends of the planks onto off-cuts of wood. It took a long time, but he was determined to make the *o*'s completely round and the curves on the *s*'s even. Eventually he could write all the letters from memory. Then in September 1829, a wonderful thing happened. The City of Baltimore opened its first public school, right in Fells Point.

There was no thought of Frederick's being enrolled in the school. No black students—even free ones—were admitted. However, Tommy Auld and several of Frederick's white friends started attending. This eventually gave Frederick access to two things he longed for—a copybook and someone to show him how to write sentences.

Five-year-old Tommy was a quick learner. Before long he'd completed his first copybook, and after showing all her friends, Miss Sophia stored it in a cupboard in the parlor. Frederick wasted no time in borrowing the copybook and taking it up to his tiny attic bedroom. Late at night, by the light of a tallow candle, he traced Tommy's writing. And when allowed outside alone in the evenings, Frederick took with him a slice of bread he'd saved from his dinner. He used the bread to entice his friends to give him writing lessons or, as the "prize" in competitions, to see who could write the longest word. Using these two methods, Frederick learned alongside the boys who attended Baltimore Public School Number 1.

Frederick was fascinated with words, collecting them wherever he could find them. Once he found some pages torn from a Bible lying in a muddy puddle. He brought them home, rinsed them, and left them to dry in the attic. They became a treasured possession, as did selected newspaper pages Hugh Auld left out to light the pitch fire at the shipyard. But the book that caught his imagination more than any other was *The Columbian Orator,* a standard text used by many schools across the northern United States. Frederick first became aware of it when two of his friends had to memorize pages from it for school.

Bill Cordery showed Frederick his copy of *The Columbian Orator.* As he flicked through the 260 pages of plays, poems, and essays, Frederick was mesmerized. Although he didn't recognize many of the authors or topics, he recognized one thing—this book contained the type of knowledge Hugh Auld did not want him to possess, the sort of knowledge that would make a person unfit to be a slave.

Frederick knew immediately he must have his own copy of the book. Just a few weeks later as he walked past Nathaniel Knight's bookstore on Thames Street, he decided to go inside. He walked in boldly and asked if the store had a used copy of *The Columbian Orator.* Nathaniel assured him that he did have the book and that it cost fifty cents. Now Frederick had something to aim for. In the evenings he shined shoes to earn the money. Soon he had his own copy of *The Columbian Orator* tucked away in a nook behind his bed. He studied the book at every opportunity, learning the same passages Bill Cordery had memorized, reading poems aloud until he understood them, and struggling through essays about freedom, moral behavior—and most astonishingly—slavery.

Of all eighty-four written pieces collected in *The Columbian Orator,* the one that spoke directly to Frederick's heart was titled "Dialogue Between a Master and a Slave." In this, for the first time, Frederick read about things he longed to be true, things he didn't even have the words to describe out loud. The narrative was a conversation between a slave owner and his slave, with the slave owner arguing that he is a "good" master because he tries to be fair to all his slaves and so his slaves should be grateful and not try to run away. The young slave he is addressing replies, "You have done nothing for me more than for your working cattle. Are they not well fed and tended? Do you work them harder than your slaves? Is not the rule of treating both designed only for your advantage? You treat both your men and beasts and slaves better than some of your neighbors because you are more prudent and wealthy than they."

"You might add more humane too," the master says.

To this the slave says, "Humane! Does it deserve that appellation to keep your fellow men in forced subjection, deprived of all exercise of their free will, liable to all the injuries that your own caprice, or the brutality of your overseers, may heap on them, and devoted, soul and body, only to your pleasure and emolument? Can gratitude take place between creatures in such a state, and the tyrant who holds them in it? Look at these limbs; are they not those of a man? Think that I have the spirit of a man too."

"Suppose I were to restore you to your liberty, would you reckon that a favor?" the master replies.

To this the slave responds, "The greatest, for although it would only be undoing a wrong, I know too well how few among mankind are capable of sacrificing interest to justice, not to prize the exertion when it is made."

As he read, Frederick stumbled over how to pronounce many of the words. He also didn't know the meaning of many other words, but he looked them up in a battered copy of *Webster's American Spelling Book* that he'd also smuggled into the house.

Sometimes in the attic at night as Frederick read essays and plays in *The Columbian Orator,* he was aware of the rhythmic thud of footsteps, the dragging of chains, and the groans of men, women, and children as they were herded down Philpot Street to the docks. The people were slaves, newly auctioned off at the Pratt Street Slave Pen and on their way south under cover of darkness so the residents of Baltimore didn't have to witness their distress. Frederick's stomach knotted every time he heard these processions pass. He couldn't help wondering if some of those passing slaves were his relatives who had met this terrifying fate.

As Frederick entered his teenage years, his view of the world expanded fast. Sunday mornings, Miss Sophia, a devout Methodist, allowed him to venture out to any church he chose to attend. As a result, the Methodist hymnal was added to his stash of books to read, memorize, and copy portions of.

Most of the time Frederick knew that the people he met assumed he was a free black boy. It made sense, since about fifteen thousand black people were living in Baltimore, and only thirty-five hundred of them were enslaved. The rest were free. Besides, Frederick was well-spoken, and with the help of *The Columbian Orator,* he knew more about the world than his educated white friends.

By 1831, thirteen-year-old Frederick attended two churches regularly. Both were Methodist churches—one mainly for white folk, and the other Bethel African Methodist Episcopal (AME) Church with its black congregation. Charles Johnson was a lay preacher at Bethel, and Frederick was captivated by his oratory. It sent him back to the introduction to *The Columbian Orator,* which explained how to speak well in public and helped him figure out just how Charles Johnson made such an impact when he spoke. Something stirred deep inside Frederick when Charles preached about how God did not want anyone to travel through the world alone, and how each person had to decide whether or not to accept Jesus Christ into his or her life.

Frederick wrestled with the idea of asking for religious salvation. He wanted to believe but understood it would change who he was and how he should behave. Was he ready to forgive the Aulds, the Anthonys, and the Lloyds for their roles in keeping him enslaved and separating him from his family?

After several weeks, Frederick decided he would become a Christian. He went forward during a service at Bethel AME Church to declare his new faith. His mind burst with possibilities. He felt surrounded by supernatural love—enough love to flow over to Hugh Auld!

In the enthusiasm of his new faith, Frederick made friends with a saintly old man, Charles Lawson, who also attended the Bethel church. Charles was a drayman at a ropewalk near the Aulds' home, and Frederick loved him like a father. The two spent as much time together as they could. Because Charles Lawson could read only a few words, Frederick would read aloud passages from the Bible, and then they would discuss them and pray together. Their friendship gave Frederick great hope. Charles often said that he believed Frederick would one day be free and that he had a powerful destiny ahead of him. Frederick doubted this was possible, arguing that he was enslaved for life. To this Charles would respond, "Trust in the Lord. The Lord can make you free. All things are possible with Him."

Frederick tried hard to believe he would be a free man one day, but events soon made this seem unlikely. Frederick was glad he could read the newspaper for himself. Otherwise he would have had to rely upon rumors about what had happened that summer two hundred miles south in Southampton County, Virginia. In early August 1831, an enslaved black preacher named Nat Turner came to believe that God had told him to lead a rebellion against white slaveholders. He and seventy followers killed over sixty white people, including many women and children. In defense and retaliation, local militias killed over one hundred black people. Another fifty were executed after being tried for taking part in the rebellion. Nat Turner escaped and was on the run for two months before being found, tried, and hanged.

Frederick was greatly disturbed by news of the rebellion. He did not condone murder, but also didn't believe in keeping people in bondage for their entire lives. He wondered which was worse.

In response to the events in Virginia, lawmakers in Maryland worked to make sure such a rebellion wouldn't happen in their state. By the end of 1831, they had tightened the laws around free black people, fearing that their lives offered hope to their enslaved brothers. Black people were no longer allowed to vote or serve in office. Any slaves who had been manumitted (freed by their owners) had to leave the state unless they gained special permission from a court to stay. Free black people from other states could no longer move to Maryland, and any free black person who didn't have a job could be re-enslaved and sold south or sent back to Africa. Frederick had read about the Maryland State Colonization Society, which the State of Maryland had been funding with ten thousand dollars annually for twenty-six years. The sole aim of this group was to entice free blacks and former slaves to leave the United States and "return" to Liberia on the west coast of Africa. The group encouraged slave owners who were becoming nervous about owning slaves to send them far away to Africa.

Frederick shook his head in disbelief at such a thing. He remembered Grandma Betsy telling him how her family had been living on Maryland's Eastern Shore for a hundred years or more. That was his mother's side, but Frederick had been told that his father's side of the family were white. How could it be that he was supposed to think of Africa as his home? Frederick had deeper family roots in America than many of the men who were passing these laws intended to send black people "home" to Africa.

In early 1833, Frederick was astonished to see his thirteen-year-old cousin Henny standing on the Aulds' doorstep waiting to be let in. He soon learned that their owner, Thomas Auld, had sent her to live in Baltimore with his brother, Hugh, since she was of no use to anyone on the Eastern Shore with her burned, crippled hands.

Hugh Auld was furious about her unexpected arrival. Frederick overheard him ranting about how he couldn't afford another useless mouth to feed. After all, he now had five children to feed and clothe, including a toddler named Wilson and baby Richard, and another baby was on the way. Henny, he declared, would have to go right back where she came from.

Frederick was nervous when Henny was sent back. He didn't think that Thomas Auld would be happy about being crossed by his younger brother.

One evening, two weeks after Henny left, Miss Sophia beckoned Frederick into the parlor. She held a letter in her shaking hands as she said, "I am sorry to say, but the Henny affair has not played out well. Mr. Thomas is very angry that Henny was returned and has just written to say that since we would not keep Henny, we cannot keep you either. You are to go back to live with him and Miss Rowena in St. Michaels."

Frederick's heart dropped. He was going to again be shipped back across Chesapeake Bay. Was this how things were going to be for the rest of his life, lurching from hope to hopelessness and back again and never finding the solid ground of freedom?

Chapter 5

Breaking Point

Every morning and evening Frederick was forced to join the Covey family for worship in the kitchen of their home on Hatton Farm. Edward Covey would read a chapter of the Bible and choose a hymn for them to sing. Frederick had a deep baritone voice, and his new master often asked him to lead the singing, which Frederick hated. He felt sick to his stomach hearing the man sing the hymns that Frederick had learned at Bethel AME Church in Baltimore. It seemed wrong to him for Edward to sing about love, brotherly unity, and finding rest for weary souls. If there was one reason Frederick was troubled and unable to find rest for his soul, it was because of Edward's bad temper and sadistic punishments. Frederick was sometimes so angry he refused to sing at all during worship, silently daring his master to beat him. At other times he mumbled the words deliberately off-key.

However pious the Coveys were during family devotions, Edward's hatred of Frederick seemed to grow daily. Frederick and Bill Smith, another slave on the farm, developed an elaborate system to warn each other when their master was near. But sometimes this was all but impossible. Edward, whom they nicknamed The Snake, seemed to Frederick to delight in keeping his slaves off balance. He would saddle up his horse and head out to St. Michaels, only to turn down a side lane and return secretly to spy on Frederick and Bill. If they slowed down in their chores or stopped to chat, he would leap out from behind a fence and lash at them with a whip. Sometimes he would crawl through a cornfield unseen and lie in wait for Frederick or Bill to take a break. If they did, Edward would jump to his feet in a violent frenzy directed at the slaves.

The only moments that lifted Frederick's spirit came when he worked in the field beside Chesapeake Bay. He would look out at Poplar Island and at the majestic ships sailing by—schooners, barques, and Baltimore clippers from all corners of the globe—and envy those who sailed on them. The vessels came and went from some of the most important ports in the world. The ships were free, and Frederick wished he could be magically transported onto their decks, transformed into a man who could chart his own destiny. But always at moments such as these a shout from Edward Covey would bring him back to grim reality.

Frederick often questioned how naïve he was to believe that one day he would be a free man, free to read and write, free to earn his own money, free to plan his own future, free to have his own wife and children he could provide for and protect.

The vicious cycle of slavery ate away at Frederick's soul, until eventually he gave up all hope. On Sundays, when the Coveys attended the local Methodist church, Frederick would usually lie under a tree staring at the sky. He didn't have the energy to go to church or the desire to sing hymns about love and brotherhood.

As a strong young slave, Frederick knew he had to be careful. He had to always appear subservient, "yes sirring" and "no sirring" his master with his eyes cast down and shoulders forward. But Frederick also knew he was at a breaking point. It was becoming harder for him to bend and scrape to Edward's demands. He knew that one day he was going to explode with uncontrolled anger. Then there would be no telling what he might do.

That day came in August when he'd been at Hatton Farm for eight months. It was the height of summer—wheat-threshing time—and Edward forced Frederick, Bill Smith, and two hired hands to work sixteen hours a day. One day, about midafternoon, Frederick felt dizzy. The sweat poured from him while his arms and legs shook uncontrollably. He staggered over to a fence and fell against it. Seconds later, he felt a sharp pain in his side. "Get up," Edward snarled. "No time for laziness! Get up and do your work." Frederick felt another jolt as his master's boot again connected with his ribs. Frederick groaned. He didn't have the strength or the will to go on. His fate was out of his hands. Edward grumbled some more and then left him there in the shade.

Frederick groaned in pain. After about ten minutes he felt a little stronger but had no desire to go back to work. Instead, he eyed the distant gate and, beyond it, the woods. Frederick rested a few more minutes, all the while watching for the moment Edward would turn the other way. When he did, with supreme effort Frederick stood and bolted toward the open gate. "Get my horse," Frederick heard Edward yell behind him as he plunged into the undergrowth beyond the gate.

Frederick ran for several minutes before he had to stop. He listened carefully. No one was following him. He sat down to think. He was a runaway, but now that he'd broken free from his master, was it possible to keep going? He looked down. He was barefoot, and his shirt was soaked with blood from where he'd been kicked. The first white person who saw him would raise the alarm. What could he do? Where could he go? He decided his best hope was to find Thomas Auld and show him how Edward had injured him. After all, Frederick was still Thomas's personal property, and he reasoned that his owner would not want him mistreated the way he had been at Hatton Farm. A healthy young male slave such as Frederick was worth eight hundred dollars, but if Edward beat him to the point where he was permanently injured, he might not be worth even half that much.

Frederick stumbled on through the underbrush toward St. Michaels. He dared not use the road. Hungry and sore, he pressed on, stopping when he had to. It took him until early evening to cover the seven miles to town, and he was relieved when the outline of the rooftops and chimneys of St. Michaels came into sight through the bushes. At the edge of town, he gathered his energy and then made a run for the general store, where he found Thomas stacking bags of beans near the counter. Thomas looked up as the door opened, and Frederick thought he saw an expression of shock cross his face, followed by a flicker of sympathy. But if that was what he saw, it didn't last long. "What are you doing here?" his owner demanded. Frederick told him the whole sorry story of life at Hatton Farm.

"Can I come back?" Frederick asked Thomas. "If I return to the farm, there's no telling what Edward Covey will do to me. His temper knows no bounds."

Thomas stood tall. His eyes narrowed. "You get yourself back there and take whatever punishment Mr. Covey—Master Covey to you—finds fit to give you. You're there to work, not lie about. No wonder he beat you. You're too haughty for your own good. You think you can take a rest while others work?"

Frederick lowered his eyes. He should have known better. No slave owner was ever going to side with him against one of his fellows. What had he been thinking?

"It's too late now. You'll have to start back first thing in the morning," his owner told him.

Frederick nodded. He supposed he would have to leave. What option did he have?

The following morning Frederick retraced his steps to Hatton Farm, keeping off the road. He feared what might happen if Edward rode up on his horse and whipped him while still mounted. It would be best if there were no surprises when he had to see his master again.

As Frederick neared the farm, he grew more afraid of what he was returning to. He climbed over a fence railing and immediately felt the sting of a whip across his back. Edward had been waiting for him. Instinctively, Frederick broke into a run and lunged into a cornfield. He crawled along until he made his way back to the boundary line and the tangle of undergrowth. His heart pounded as he tried to decide what to do. But no answer came. Twenty-four hours later, hunger drew him back once again to the Covey farm.

By now it was Sunday morning, and Frederick arrived just in time to see the Covey family leaving for church. They waved cheerfully. "Good to see you, Frederick. One of the pigs escaped from the sty. Could you round him up for me?" Edward asked rather than demanded.

Frederick nodded. If his master were a rational man, this change of behavior would have been strange, but Frederick knew that Edward Covey practiced his best behavior on Sundays. All sorts of things could not be done on the Lord's Day. One of those things was whipping slaves. That would have to wait until Monday.

Early the next morning Edward ordered Frederick to go to the stables to feed and rub down the horses. This surprised Frederick. It was no longer Sunday, and he'd assumed that the first thing his master would do was whip him hard for running away. However, it didn't take long for Edward's wrath to overcome him. As Frederick stood on a ladder pulling hay down from the loft to feed the horses, his master grabbed him and threw him to the ground. Frederick was caught off guard, but when Edward tried to tie up his feet, something exploded within him, welled up like a rushing spring—the urge to fight back. Frederick's body already bore the familiar hatch-mark scars from whippings and beatings from Edward Covey, and Frederick wasn't going to let his master do that to him again.

At sixteen years of age, Frederick was taller than Edward, and he kicked away from his master so he couldn't tie up his ankles. As Frederick jumped to his feet, Edward charged at him, trying to tackle him and drag him back down to the stable floor. But Frederick resisted his lunge and accompanying flurry of punches. He had no time to think about what he was doing. He just reacted while trying to avoid Edward's frenzied attacks. When Bill Hughes, Edward's cousin who worked on the farm, saw what was happening, he rushed to help his relative. But as he approached, Frederick let forth a powerful kick that connected with Bill's groin. Bill quickly left the fight and slumped to the ground in agony.

On and on the fighting went, with Frederick resisting his master's attempts to restrain him at every turn. It was clear to Frederick that he had the upper hand in the struggle and that Edward, sweating and breathing heavily from the exertion, was tiring. When Bill Smith, another slave whose master had contracted for him to work at Hatton Farm, arrived back from a visit with his family, Edward called to him to come and help him subdue Frederick. Bill replied politely, "Mr. Covey, I want to go to work."

"This is your work! Take hold of him," Edward huffed.

Frederick saw Bill look at him before telling Edward, "My master hired me here to work and not to help you whip Frederick." With that, Bill walked away.

The fight moved from inside the stable to the cow pen. Edward made another charge, and Frederick grabbed him and threw him headlong to the ground. Edward's head landed in a pile of cow dung. On and on it went. Neither man was willing to give up. When the fight finally ground to a halt, both men were gasping for air. Edward looked at Frederick and pointed to the barn. "Now, you scoundrel, go to your work. I would not have whipped you half as much as I did had you not resisted."

Frederick looked at his master, who was covered with blood and cow dung. He knew that Edward's words were meant only to try to save face. After all, Edward hadn't whipped him or even managed to draw blood on Frederick's body.

After the fight, Frederick noticed his master avoided him as much as possible. He would tell him what to do and then leave him to get the job done in his own way. Even when Frederick goaded him, Edward wouldn't whip him. Frederick tried to think of an explanation for this change. Was his master afraid of him? Or had Thomas Auld intervened to stop his "property" from being abused any further? Either way, Frederick was glad to have some respite from Edward's brutality.

Things continued to improve for Frederick. Once his yearlong contract working at Hatton Farm expired at Christmas 1834, he was transferred to a new farm closer to St. Michaels. Frederick was one of five workers on a property that bordered the Miles River. The farm was owned by William Freeland, Rowena Auld's uncle. Frederick liked him. He was fair, fed his slaves well, allowed them to rest and recuperate when they were hurt, and did not pry into what they did on their own time.

Of the four other slaves working on the Freeland farm, three of them, brothers Henry and John Harris and Handy Caldwell, were all around Frederick's age, while Sandy Jenkins was an older man. As they talked, Frederick discovered that the Harris brothers were eager to learn to read and write, and he was equally eager to teach them. While it wasn't illegal to teach slaves to read or write in Maryland as it was in most of the Southern states, Frederick knew from experience many white people living on the Eastern Shore didn't take kindly to the idea. If they were careful and undertook their lessons away from prying white eyes, he felt he could succeed teaching the other slaves on the farm to read and write.

The group, including Sandy Jenkins, met on Sunday mornings when most white people throughout the area were attending church. They met under a spreading live oak tree on the riverbank or in the back of the barn if it was too cold or wet outside. Frederick used three books to teach from: his beloved copy of *The Columbian Orator*, which he'd managed to keep hidden from the Aulds and Edward Covey, *Webster's American Spelling Book*, and a Bible.

Although the Sunday morning school went unnoticed by most whites, other slaves took note. Within months more than thirty of them from nearby farms quietly made their way by various routes to the outdoor schoolhouse on the Freeland farm.

Teaching these people to read and write and, most of all, envision a different future for themselves filled Frederick with a pride he'd never felt before. He studied the introduction to *The Columbian Orator*, which gave instructions on how to speak better. He learned about the importance of pronouncing words correctly, about the cadence of language, how to emphasize words, and how to gesture while speaking. During each lesson Frederick taught at Sunday morning school, he put this advice into practice. He would also give spirited readings about various topics and ideas from *The Columbian Orator*. Although many of the ideas were far above what his students could understand, Frederick believed they should be exposed to lofty ideals. One day they would not just hear about freedom but might actually experience it for themselves.

Chapter 6

Band of Brothers

Frederick worked hard to instill the hope of freedom to those attending his school, yet as he did so, freedom seemed to be slipping further from his grasp. In January 1836, he came to realize he'd been lulled by the rhythm of working on the Freeland farm. Yes, William Freeland was a "good" master, but Frederick reminded himself he was a master nonetheless and had complete control over his life. If he was going to be free and master of his own life, Frederick was going to have to take action—decisive action.

Seventeen-year-old Frederick ran through many escape scenarios from the Eastern Shore. Could he escape by land? At its narrowest, the neck of land between the Miles River and the Choptank River was less than three-quarters of a mile wide. All the slave owners would have to do was create a line across the land between the rivers and wait for him to try to cross. But what about escaping by boat? Frederick had never heard of anyone doing that. Could it work? What kind of boat would he use? How would he know if the tides and currents would take him all the way to the head of Chesapeake Bay? From there it would be a half day's walk to Pennsylvania, where he would at last be free.

Frederick cautiously approached his best friends on the Freeland farm—Henry and John Harris, Sandy Jenkins, and Charles Roberts and Henry Bailey (who both lived on William Hambleton's farm next door). Henry Bailey was technically Frederick's uncle, even though he was the younger of the two. The group discussed the idea of escaping from the Eastern Shore by boat, and all agreed it might just work. More important, they committed to be a part of the escape attempt. Sandy Jenkins, who was much older than the rest of them and married to a free woman who had her own cabin near the Covey farm, liked the idea too. He told Frederick that after they escaped and reached Pennsylvania, he planned to communicate with his wife so she could join him there and they could start a new, free life together.

The band of brothers, as Frederick thought of them, met under the stars whenever they could to discuss details of their plan. Even though he was the second to youngest member of the band, Frederick was their obvious leader.

William Hambleton kept a large canoe on the riverbank at his farm, less than a quarter mile from the Freeland property. The band of brothers decided they could steal it. Paddling seemed much easier to them than sailing. But what if the canoe was intercepted? How could they explain six black men paddling a boat unsupervised in the open water of Chesapeake Bay?

For every question they came up with a solution. Free blacks carried papers with them at all times, and enslaved blacks who were far from their masters also needed to carry papers so that they could show they had permission to travel. Frederick would forge permission papers for them all, a serious crime if the person was caught—and one reason why many masters didn't want their slaves to become literate. The men saved food for the journey, and Sandy Jenkins got them flasks for storing fresh water.

Sometimes their plans carried an air of certainty, while at other times the men spiraled into despair. What if a big wave hit them out on the bay and they were capsized? What if they were followed in a faster vessel and recaptured? If that happened, they would most certainly be sold south into a much more dire situation than their current one. To keep everyone's spirits up, Frederick often recited the last part of Patrick Henry's speech that had helped to start the Revolutionary War sixty years before. The British colonies in North America were faced with unreasonable demands from their overlords. When Patrick Henry rose to speak before the Second Virginia Convention in 1775, he argued for revolt—even at the cost of their own lives:

> There is no longer any room for hope. If we wish to be free, we must fight! I repeat it, sir, we must fight! An appeal to arms and to the God of hosts is all that is left us!
>
> It is in vain, sir, to extenuate the matter. The war is actually begun! Our brethren are already in the field! Why stand we here idle? Is life so dear, or peace so sweet, as to be purchased at the price of chains and slavery? Forbid it, Almighty God! I know not what course others may take; but as for me, give me liberty or give me death!

Frederick encouraged the men to do all they could to flee peacefully, but if necessary they needed to do whatever it took to gain their freedom. He told them that if Patrick Henry was offended over taxes and import regulations, how much more should black slaves be militant that their lives had been stolen from them. They could be lashed, chained, starved, or abused by their masters and owners without consequence. Frederick reminded the band of brothers that they, just as the American colonists, had the right to fight for their own future.

The evening of Saturday, April 2, 1836, was chosen as the night on which they would escape. It was the night before Easter Sunday, when white people would be distracted with family celebrations.

The week before their escape, Sandy Jenkins pulled out of the scheme. He said he'd had dreams that left him with a bad feeling about the escape plan. Frederick was disappointed but understood.

Sandy had a good life there and a wife he would have to leave behind. Although she was free and couldn't be sold south as punishment for her husband's crime of freeing himself, she could easily lose her job and her livelihood.

By the time the sun came up on Saturday morning, the day of the escape, Frederick and Sandy were shoveling manure in the home field. All at once as they worked side by side, Frederick felt his spirit sag. He didn't know why, but in a split second he was convinced the band of brothers had been betrayed and the white masters knew of their plan. He turned to Sandy and said, "We are betrayed. Something just told me so."

Sandy looked at him curiously. "Man, dat is strange, but I think so too."

When the horn for breakfast blew and he walked with Sandy and the Harris brothers toward the Freeland's kitchen, Frederick felt sick to his stomach. Sandy and Henry Harris walked on to the barn to put away their shovels, while Frederick and John Harris entered the kitchen. As he glanced out the kitchen window, Frederick saw William Hambleton on horseback galloping up the lane to the Freeland house. Through a gap in the trees, he could see four more men on horseback riding up the lane behind him. Frederick's stomach lurched as he watched William Freeland walk out of the barn to meet his hastily arriving neighbor. Once William Hambleton had dismounted, the two men held a quick conversation and then headed straight toward the kitchen. As they did so, the four men on horseback, who turned out to be constables, rode up beside the kitchen. Charles Roberts and Henry Bailey, their hands tied, were being led along one by one to the mounted constables. Frederick's premonition of betrayal had been right. What hope did they have now?

Before Frederick could react, two constables burst into the kitchen, grabbed Frederick and John Harris, and dragged them outside, where they tied the men's hands. Given the speed with which the constables seized Frederick and tied him up, all thought of resistance evaporated. *So much for "give me liberty or give me death,"* Frederick thought ruefully as he waited for what would happen next. Another constable dragged Henry from the barn, but Henry resisted with all his might, struggling with the constable and refusing to allow his hands to be tied. Another constable rushed to help, drawing his pistol, cocking it, and aiming point-blank at Henry's chest. Still Henry would not give up the fight. Looking the constable in the eye, he said, "Shoot! Shoot me now! I won't go with you to be tried." Soon all four constables attacked Henry and dragged him to the ground, where they managed to get his hands tied. As he watched this happen, Frederick was impressed by Henry's courage and defiance. He also used the constables' distraction with Henry to throw his forged travel permission paper into the nearby fire.

Frederick and the other two men were marched over and tied to the horses, joining Charles Roberts and Henry Bailey. The constables mounted up and began the fifteen-mile journey to the jail in Easton. The captured men marched along beside them. As they departed, Betsy Freeland, William Freeland's mother and William Hambleton's sister, ran up to Frederick and screamed at him, "You devil! You put the idea of freedom and the notion to run away into their heads." Frederick said nothing and just walked on.

Along the way to Easton, other white people came to watch the procession. They jeered and shouted that Frederick should be hanged for his treachery. Frederick kept his head down and moved along silently. But inside he screamed, *Why? What have I done to deserve such an end except seek the freedom and dignity reserved for human beings? All I want is to control my own destiny, just as you control yours.*

As the miles passed, the captured men took the opportunity to whisper to each other. Frederick urged them to eat their forged travel passes so they would not be found. Frederick also told them that when they reached the jail and were interrogated, they should deny everything and admit to nothing.

At the jail in Easton, Frederick sat on a stone bench, head in his hands, and pondered what had happened. In the space of eight hours, he'd gone from the soaring hope of freedom to the confines of a prison cell and the certainty that he would be sold to a Southern plantation, where his reputation would precede him. He would be known as the ringleader in an escape plan and be singled out for harsh treatment. The letter R for runaway would probably be branded on his forehead. Of course, if the forged travel passes had been found, Frederick would be facing death.

Easter Sunday dawned. Bitterness rose in Frederick as he looked out the arched, barred cell window. By now he was meant to be paddling up Chesapeake Bay, every dip of the paddle taking him closer to freedom. Instead, he was in jail watching Easton come alive. Already families, the men in their best suits and women in flowing dresses and sporting Easter bonnets, were walking or riding to church in buggies. Meanwhile Frederick knew that slaves up and down Maryland's Eastern Shore would be getting out their owners' best china and arranging it on polished tables while lamb and venison roasted in the kitchen as pies and sweetmeats were being prepared. When their masters and families returned from Easter Sunday church services, there would be a bountiful feast. But there would be nothing for Frederick, who was locked up in a jail cell facing a grim future.

On Monday morning the doors of the cell swung open and slave buyers from the South swaggered in. They demanded that Frederick and the others open their mouths for inspection. They felt the men's muscles and made them walk to check for limps and flat feet. Still, by the end of the week none of them had been sold. This gave the five plenty of time to think about who it was that had betrayed them. Frederick thought it must have been Sandy Jenkins, though he could hardly believe that his friend would do that. Yet no one else had been aware of their plans, especially the forged travel passes Frederick had made that the prison warden seemed to be looking for.

Finally, William Hambleton and William Freeland arrived at the jail. They took away the Harris brothers, along with Charles Roberts and Henry Bailey. Frederick was left alone in the cell. A week passed, but Thomas Auld did not show up at the prison to retrieve him. Surely, Frederick concluded, his master was making final plans to sell him south.

Chapter 7

Too Good to Be True

Frederick heard a key turn. The cell door creaked open. The warden stepped aside, and Thomas Auld appeared. "Get up," he ordered. "What a sorry mess you've made of things, Frederick," he added, beckoning Frederick to follow him.

Soon Frederick was back at the Auld home in St. Michaels. It was a gloomy place to be. Thomas told him he would be sold to a friend in Alabama—and quickly—since William Hambleton had declared he would shoot Frederick if he saw his face in Talbot County again. However, three days after his release from jail, Frederick learned that Thomas had other plans for him. "I'm sending you back to my brother Hugh in Baltimore," he announced gruffly. "I'll instruct him to find you a trade to learn. If you behave well and don't cause trouble, I'll free you in seven years."

Frederick frowned. Had he heard correctly? Was he really being sent back to Baltimore with the possibility of being freed? It seemed too good to be true. But sure enough, for the third time in his life, Frederick found himself sailing back across Chesapeake Bay from Maryland's Eastern Shore.

Many things had changed in Baltimore in the three years that Frederick had been away. Hugh Auld's shipbuilding venture had failed. As a result, the Auld family now lived in a cheaper house and Hugh worked as an overseer at Price's shipyard. Ten years earlier when Frederick first arrived at the Auld home, two-year-old Tommy had peered at him from behind his mother's skirt. Back then he was their only child. Now there were six Auld children, with the recent birth of baby Edward. Frederick could see that the past three years had taken a toll on Miss Sophia, who seemed worn down with work and worry.

The younger children didn't remember Frederick, and he felt out of place being back at the Auld home. He was no longer a boy ready to be molded to the needs of a white family. Now he was an eighteen-year-old young man, six feet one inch tall, powerfully built, and accustomed to spending his days among men in the fields. Even though Sophia Auld seemed to have more housework than ever, it was obvious to Frederick that they needed his income more than his household help. He was soon hired out to William Gardiner's shipyard to learn the trade of caulking.

Frederick had previously worked in Hugh Auld's shipyard, where he often worked alongside the caulkers. His most hated job was picking oakum for caulkers to use. As a result, he had a good idea of what to expect. In a shipyard that built new vessels, it was the job of caulkers to seal the gaps between the wooden planks of the new ship's hull and decks, making them leak-free and watertight. It was a skilled job that involved forcing cotton yarn or string and oakum into the gaps using special tools and mallets. Once this was in place, the material was sealed over with a layer of pitch and then painted with a thick layer of white lead paint. Since the new ships being built were not yet in the water, the caulker's job was much cleaner and more straightforward than recaulking older ships that had already been to sea.

Spring 1836, as Frederick soon learned, was one of the worst times for a defiant young slave to be entering the shipbuilding trade in Baltimore. Over the previous few years, white immigrants, especially single men from Ireland, had poured into the city. Most lacked work skills and competed openly with the free black men of Baltimore who had worked in the trades there for many years. When Frederick arrived at Gardiner's shipyard, it had a very different feel from the shipyard Hugh Auld and Edward Harrison had run. Working conditions at Gardiner's shipyard were laced with racial tension because of the new Irish immigrants who had been hired. Added to this was the fact that shipbuilding at Gardiner's was rolling along on a breakneck pace. When Frederick arrived, they were building two man-o-wars for the Mexican government, both running behind schedule.

"Do what any of them tell you—as quick as you can," Mr. Gardiner told Frederick on his first day at the shipyard. Frederick knew that this would be a challenge, if not an impossibility. Seventy-five tradesmen worked in the shipyard, all of whom wanted Frederick at their beck and call.

Sure enough, Frederick's days were filled with commands: "Get me more oakum." "Fill that paint bucket quickly." "Hold the end of this plank while I saw it." On and on the demands went. No matter how hard Frederick worked to fulfill them, the white men at the shipyard always seemed to be angry at him. Frederick soon learned that their anger wasn't directed solely at him but toward all the black workers at the shipyard, even skilled tradesmen.

Everyone at Gardiner's shipyard labored under pressure to complete the two warships on schedule. One day, the white carpenters put down their tools and walked off the job, announcing to Mr. Gardiner that they would not return unless he fired all the black carpenters. Frederick watched as the situation unfolded. What would happen as a result of the carpenters' actions? Mr. Gardiner faced serious financial penalties if the ships weren't finished on time, and there were many more white carpenters than black ones employed at his shipyard. Bowing to the pressure, Mr. Gardiner fired all the black carpenters, and the white carpenters returned to work triumphant.

Frederick soon felt the effects of this chilling change. With no older black men around to watch out for him, he worked under constant fear. The immigrant workers yelled and laughed at him and set impossible tasks for him to do. They even tripped and kicked him as he went about his tasks. Every morning Frederick had to return to the abusive shipyard to earn money he was obligated to hand over to Hugh Auld.

One day as Frederick went about his work at Gardiner's shipyard, four white apprentices surrounded him and attacked him with bricks and a heavy handspike. As Frederick fought to defend himself from the apprentices, one of them cracked the handspike down on his head. Stunned by the blow he fell to the ground. The four apprentices descended upon him, beating him with their fists. As Frederick curled into a ball, he became aware that most of the fifty white carpenters had joined in, yelling "Kill him! Kill him!" in unison.

As soon as Frederick's strength and focus returned, he pushed himself onto his hands and knees. One of the apprentices kicked Frederick hard. His heavy boot connected with Frederick's left eye, which erupted with a gush of blood. Frederick thought his eyeball must have exploded from the force. The apprentices stopped, and Frederick assumed that they were satisfied with what they'd done to him. He could have walked away, but at that moment he saw his chance to even the score. Despite the blood and the pain he felt, Frederick leapt to his feet, grabbed a handspike, and lunged at the four apprentices, who fled. Frederick raced after them, but the carpenters stepped in and blocked

Frederick's path. Instead, Frederick turned and stumbled home to the Auld house.

Frederick saw how shocked the Aulds were at his condition. Instead of harsh words for him, they responded with care and sympathy. Miss Sophia sat on a chair in front of him and tenderly bathed his wounds and wiped away the blood. Then she took a slab of fresh lean beef and placed it over his swollen left eye. Meanwhile, Hugh asked Frederick about what had happened to him. When he found out, he seemed genuinely incensed at the way his slave had been treated.

Two days later, still angry about the attack, Hugh took Frederick with him to visit the local justice of the peace to have charges laid against the four apprentices. He soon discovered what Frederick already knew; what his cousin Tom had explained to him when he was seven years old back on the Wye Plantation: there was no justice for a black man—slave or free—to be had. Esquire Watson explained to Hugh and Frederick that the law in Maryland was clear: no black person could testify against a white person. It didn't matter that Frederick, still battered and bruised from the attack, could give a firsthand account of the events that took place. He was a black man, and his account meant nothing in the eyes of the law. Esquire Watson told them that if one of the white carpenters came forward to testify, charges could be laid against Frederick's attackers. Frederick knew that no one would break ranks and do that at Gardiner's shipyard. After arguing for a while, Hugh gave up on getting justice for Frederick.

Frederick knew he'd been lucky to escape the attack, but he began to fret for what might happen to him when he returned to work at Gardiner's shipyard. Next time they might kill him. He was thankful when Hugh came to the same conclusion. Not wanting to lose the income that Frederick provided the family, Hugh decided that Frederick wouldn't return to Gardiner's shipyard. Instead, Frederick would begin working at Price's shipyard where, as overseer, Hugh could help protect him.

At Price's shipyard, Frederick began to learn the caulking trade. Despite its being dirty, hard physical work, Frederick learned quickly. Soon he was able to scrape and stuff, tamp and hammer effortlessly. And while his hands were busy, his mind was free to think about more important things.

Baltimore was growing fast, with far more free blacks living in the city than enslaved. This meant that most of the other black men and women Frederick met and became friends with were free. On Sundays he began attending the Sharp Street Methodist Episcopal Church, where he liked to take notes on the inspiring sermons he heard. At the church he met a free black woman named Anna Murray. As the two talked, Frederick discovered that they had both been born on Maryland's Eastern Shore, just three miles from each other. Anna, who was five years his senior, now worked for a Mr. Wells in Baltimore. Although Frederick and Anna couldn't remember meeting each other as children, they knew many of each other's relatives and liked to reminisce about the old mill and the Tuckahoe Creek, where they had each spent many happy hours as children.

Frederick and several young, free black caulkers formed a secret debating club, which they named the East Baltimore Mental Improvement Society. They spent most Saturday nights together debating topics as far ranging as the merits of not drinking alcohol to the meaning of Christ's resurrection. Frederick enjoyed honing his speaking skills and learning from the others as they debated. He began to feel he was leading two lives, one as a slave at a shipyard and the other as an intelligent young man in Baltimore—free to think his own thoughts and pursue his own interests.

Two years passed, and Frederick's life was going well, except for one problem—he was enslaved, the legal property of another man. Although he worked hard at Price's shipyard, it was Hugh Auld who claimed his paycheck every Saturday. Sometimes Hugh gave Frederick a few pennies of the money to spend, but this infuriated him. What right did Hugh Auld have to take all the money Frederick had worked so hard for?

As Frederick left his teenage years behind, in May 1838, fifteen-year-old Tommy Auld went off to sea aboard the *Tweed.* He was setting out on life's adventure while Frederick's future appeared to be working six days a week while someone else collected his wages.

After Miss Sophia gave birth to yet another baby, Zepporah, the house seemed to be more crowded than ever, despite Tommy's departure. Frederick was surprised when Hugh told him he was willing to negotiate a different living arrangement. If Frederick showed up at the door every Saturday night with three dollars from his wages, Hugh would allow him to find his own room and board and his own job on the waterfront. And if he earned extra money above the three dollars, he could keep it. Frederick calculated that his room and board would cost two and a half dollars per week and his clothes and tools another fifty cents. He would need to earn at least six dollars a week to cover his basic needs and give his master the three dollars he demanded. If he earned any more than that, he would need to save it for those weeks when bad weather closed the shipyards or he was unable to find work. It was a gamble, but Frederick hoped that by the end of the year he would have saved enough extra money to think about making a run for freedom in the North.

Frederick was grateful for the freedoms his new living arrangement afforded him. He found a boardinghouse in which to stay, and no one questioned him as to where he was going or where he had been and why. He could attend as many meetings as he wanted and even take a day off work if he'd saved enough money. He could buy books and read them in the boardinghouse parlor in the evening or stroll down the streets on Sunday mornings with Anna instead of getting the Auld children ready for church. But every Saturday night bitterness engulfed him as he turned over the three dollars to his master. The money represented a sizeable amount of hard work, and what had Hugh Auld done to deserve it? What right did he have to the cash? None as far as Frederick could see, except that the surrounding society made it acceptable. Sometimes it was difficult for him to earn the needed amount each week, yet Frederick knew that if he didn't, he would have to go back into the Aulds' overcrowded house.

Things under the new living arrangement went as well as could be expected for three months, until Frederick used some of his money to attend a camp meeting north of Baltimore. He'd only intended to stay at the camp meeting for the day, but his friends persuaded him to stay two nights and return to Baltimore on Sunday evening. The first thing he did upon arriving back was to take three dollars to Hugh Auld. As soon as he opened the door and saw Frederick, Hugh flew into a rage. How dare Frederick treat him this way, he demanded. They had an arrangement, which he'd abused. He was over a day late paying the money he was obligated to turn over. Hugh threatened to beat him, but Frederick knew he was bigger and stronger than Hugh. Instead, his master rescinded Frederick's living arrangement. Frederick was to move back into the Auld house and could no longer hire himself out and keep part of the money he earned. Going forward, all the money Frederick earned would once more be handed over to Hugh Auld.

Frederick understood his mistake. Under the new living arrangement, he'd allowed himself to be lulled into imagining he was free, but invisible bonds held him firmly to his master. He had gone too far, and Hugh was angry with him. Yet underneath his master's bravado, Frederick realized Hugh was afraid—afraid that he had lost control of Frederick, that Frederick had run away when he had gone to the camp meeting, that he might not get to keep any more of Frederick's wages. So once more Hugh wanted to take closer control of Frederick's life. Frederick was not free. Yes, his owner, Thomas Auld, had promised him freedom when he was twenty-five. But that was five years away, and would it even really happen? All Frederick knew was that he couldn't go back to living with the Aulds. He hoped he would be able to convince Hugh that he was sorry, that he was harmless and docile and had no thoughts of his own freedom. But of course, Frederick clearly wanted his freedom more than anything else in the world.

And what about a future with Anna Murray? By now the two were in love, but as a slave, Frederick couldn't marry her, even though Anna was a free woman. So what future did they have together if he was not free? As Frederick went to work the next day, these thoughts swirled inside his head until he knew one thing for sure: he had to escape north to true freedom—and soon. He would ask Anna if she had the courage to join him.

Chapter 8

The Indescribable Feeling

Early on Monday morning, September 3, 1838, with his caulking toolbox in hand, Frederick walked out of the Auld house. He turned left into Strawberry Alley, where his friend Isaac Rolles lived, and gently knocked on his door. Isaac opened the door immediately, and the two men's eyes met. Frederick and Isaac didn't need to talk. They both knew that what they were about to do was illegal. Frederick was about to attempt to "steal" his own body—his master's property—and Isaac, a free black man, was going to help him commit the crime.

At the threshold of the door Frederick drew a deep breath, stepped inside, and set down his toolbox. If all went well, Anna Murray would take the toolbox with her when she made her own journey north in a few days. Frederick pushed that thought out of his mind. Right now he needed to harness his wits to get himself north. He needed to transform into Antoine Stanley, a free black sailor who had offered to loan Frederick his Sailor's Protection Paper. Frederick was sure he could pass himself off as a sailor. He'd spent years around shipyards and had studied how sailors talked. He also knew that black sailors were a common sight on trains and ferries, since they often had to get from one port to another to join a different ship.

Anna had sewn Frederick a sailor's outfit—brown pants, a red flannel shirt, and a black cravat that he tied loosely around his neck. She had even spilled tea on the shirt and then pounded the clothes on a washboard so they no longer looked new. He completed his outfit with a waterproof tarpaulin hat that a friend had bought for him at a nearby slopshop.

Three weeks had passed since Frederick's debacle with Hugh Auld about being late in handing over the required three dollars from his wages. Now, with the help of his friends at the East Baltimore Mental Improvement Society, his church friends, and, of course, Anna, Frederick was about to make his bid for freedom. He folded the clothes he'd been wearing and placed them into one of two small bags he was taking with him. The other bag contained his most precious possessions: his Bible, a copy of *The Columbian Orator*, and Webster's spelling book, along with some items a sailor might carry with him from port to port—a thin flannel blanket, pen, and small bottle of ink. Nothing in the bags could identify him as a runaway slave or a caulker. Closing the bags, Frederick was satisfied he'd done all he could to look like a young sailor making his way from Baltimore to New York City to join a new ship.

At six feet one inch tall, it was hard for Frederick to blend into a crowd. As a result, he knew that the short walk from Strawberry Alley to the newly finished Wilmington and Baltimore train station would likely be the most dangerous walk of his life. Anyone who recognized him wearing a sailor's outfit would instantly realize something was up and turn him in to the authorities. Isaac would bring Frederick's bags to him at the station on his dray and hand them over right before Frederick boarded the train. That way Frederick didn't need to lug the bags with him through the streets and draw more attention to himself. Keeping his head down and moving quickly, Frederick made his way to meet Anna, who was waiting at the designated meeting spot. The couple walked the last half mile to the station in silence. Anna promised that if all went well, she would join Frederick in the North, where they would marry. If things didn't go according to plan, they would likely never see each other again.

The train was due to depart the station at 8:00 a.m. Rather than present himself at the ticket window where he would have to show his papers, Frederick decided to make a dash for the train just as it was pulling out of the station. He knew a ticket collector would make his way through the train after it left, and Frederick could buy a ticket directly from him, hopefully without too many questions.

All went according to the plan. Isaac arrived as the station just as the steam engine began to hiss and wheeze. Frederick gave Anna's hand one final squeeze and grabbed his bags as the train inched forward. He ran alongside the train and leapt aboard the Negro car, where he spotted a spare seat halfway down the aisle. By the time he reached it, the train was gathering speed. He was on a journey that would define his future. Frederick knew that he was now in God's hands. This journey could end in only one of two ways. Within a few hours he would safely make it north, where he would be free, or his plan would be discovered and he would be arrested and sent south, never to see Anna or his friends again.

Without thinking, as he took his seat, Frederick thrust his right hand deep into the pocket of his sailor's pants. For reassurance, he ran his fingers along the edge of the Sailor's Protection Paper. He resisted the urge to pull the paper out, unfold it, and study it. He didn't have to. By now he knew it by heart. At the top of the page in large script was the word *Protection*, with an illustration of an American eagle beneath it and the words *United States of America*. This was a paper American seamen carried with them to prove their citizenship and claim the rights of an American wherever they happened to be—whether at sea or on land—in the world.

Unfortunately, the paper also had a description of Antoine Stanley. "This paper allows Antoine Stanley, an American Seaman aged forty-five years or thereabouts, of the height of five feet six inches, dark complexion and woolly hair born in Maryland."

Frederick sat glumly after recalling the wording of the description. He was seven inches taller than Antoine and twenty-five years younger, and his skin was several shades lighter. The only thing the two men had in common was woolly hair. If the ticket collector read the description too closely, the ruse would be over.

Frederick wouldn't have to wait long to find out what would happen when he presented the Sailor's Protection Paper. The ticket collector entered the carriage and made his way down the aisle toward Frederick. When he reached him, Frederick gave him a broad, confident smile, which elicited a similar smile from the collector. "Do you have your free papers with you?" he asked Frederick politely.

"No, sir. I never carry my free papers with me when I go to sea," he replied calmly.

"Surely you have something with you to show you are a free man."

"Yes, sir. I have my Sailor's Protection Paper with the American eagle on it, and which carries me around the world," Frederick said with fake pride. The conductor seemed impressed with his answer as he slid the paper from his pocket and handed it over. The collector unfolded the paper but barely glanced at it. The name and the American eagle at the top seemed to be all that mattered to him. He refolded the paper, handed it back to Frederick, and took the money from him for the fare. Frederick breathed a sigh of relief as the conductor moved on. He'd passed the first challenge. He was safe, at least for the moment.

Settling into his seat, Frederick looked out of the carriage window as the scenery whizzed past at twenty-five miles per hour. He'd never traveled so fast or so far north before. Although he wanted to be excited, he felt sad. He thought about everything he was leaving behind in his bid for freedom. He had been born and raised in Maryland, and all his friends lived there, as did those members of his family who hadn't been sold south. Everything he knew—his church, the members of the East Baltimore Mental Improvement Society, and Anna Murray—all lay behind him. What if Anna got cold feet and decided not to join him in New York City? He wouldn't blame her if she didn't come. What did he have to offer? Not much. He would be a runaway slave, broke, homeless, friendless, a refugee in a Northern state.

The first leg of Frederick's journey would carry him thirty-seven miles from Baltimore to Havre de Grace, Maryland, where all passengers would disembark the train and cross the Susquehanna River by ferryboat. Across the river lay a forty-mile train ride through Maryland and on to Wilmington, Delaware, another slave state. In Wilmington he would leave the train behind and walk to the docks, where he would board a steamboat and ride it up the Delaware River to Philadelphia, Pennsylvania. After docking there, Frederick would take his first long, deep breath as a free man.

As Frederick sat on the wooden bench seat on the train, his mind went back to his earlier failed escape attempt. He tried to calm himself with the thought that this time he had already gone farther away from his master than he had on that previous attempt. All he had to do now was keep his wits about him and hope he didn't encounter anyone who recognized him. He assured himself it was safer to travel alone. There was less chance of his being recognized, and if he did have to talk his way out of a situation, he didn't have to worry about anyone else's story not matching his.

On the ferryboat crossing the Susquehanna River, Frederick had to work hard to avoid a black crew member who seemed impressed by his sailor's garb and tried to ply him with questions about his life at sea. Then, on the other side of the river as Frederick sat down in his seat on the northbound train, the southbound train huffed to a halt next to them at the station. Frederick peered over at the newly arrived train. Through the window he saw Captain McGowan, whose new cutter Frederick had been working on the week before at Walter Price's shipyard. Frederick slunk low in his seat. Fortunately, Captain McGowan didn't glance out the window before disembarking the train. Frederick breathed another sigh of relief. But his relief was short-lived when he saw on his train another man—Frederick Steen, a German blacksmith who'd worked in the same shipyard as Frederick. As the train rolled along on its way to Wilmington, the blacksmith looked back at him. While no words passed between the two, Frederick was certain the German blacksmith had recognized him. Would he turn him in to the conductor? Frederick waited. The train crossed into Delaware and headed toward Wilmington. In Wilmington, Frederick Steen smiled slightly as he picked up his bag and left the train ahead of Frederick. Stepping onto the station platform, Frederick breathed still another sigh of relief. It had been a close call, and he still had miles to go to freedom.

Frederick's hands shook with fear as he walked to the docks to catch a steamboat upriver to Philadelphia. Delaware was a slave state, while neighboring Pennsylvania was a free state. Frederick had been warned that many slave hunters patrolled the borders between North and South as well as around the docks. To distract himself from fear and panic, Frederick wondered what Hugh Auld might be doing right now. It was lunchtime, and Hugh probably had no idea Frederick was missing. He wouldn't realize something was wrong until Frederick didn't show up for dinner. Would Hugh wait until morning to send out inquiries as to Frederick's whereabouts and raise the alarm that he was missing? Or would he march straight down to the shipyard to find out if Frederick had shown up for work that day? And what about Anna? She would be setting the table with silverware and fine china, in time for Mr. Wells to come home for his midday meal with his family.

Two hours later, Frederick considered how smoothly everything had gone. He had encountered no slave hunters, and when he showed the Sailor's Protection Paper to the ticket seller before boarding the steamer, the seller had barely glanced at Frederick or the paper and had wished him well on his next ship.

To Frederick the Delaware River was broad and beautiful. When he stepped from the steamer at the dock in Philadelphia, he was at last a free man! Being a person who loved words, Frederick struggled to find the right ones to describe how he felt that late afternoon. All his life he'd longed to be free, and now he stood north of the Mason-Dixon Line. He was free! The feeling was indescribable, beyond words.

With some money left in his pocket, Frederick decided to continue moving north to New York City, another hundred miles northeast. He asked a black man standing on a street corner how he might get to New York. The man directed him to Willow Street Railway Station and told him to take the overnight train from the station to the line's terminus in Hoboken, New Jersey. From there he should catch a ferryboat across the Hudson River to New York.

At daybreak on September 4, 1838, Frederick stood at the bow of the ferry as it steamed across the Hudson River from Hoboken to the foot of Chambers Street in Manhattan. New York City was grand. Buildings that glowed red in the early morning sunlight were everywhere, and people bustled about. "Mind your step," the ticket collector said as he pulled a metal gate to one side. As Frederick stepped from the ferry into the busy world of New York City, his emotions bombarded him. He felt more alone than ever, elated that he'd kept his wits about him long enough to be free, awed by the enormity of what lay ahead, and very afraid all at the same time.

Frederick gripped his bags tightly as he walked away from the dock at the bottom of Chambers Street toward the buildings. Everyone around him seemed to have something to do—except him. He was anxious to explore this new city, unlike anything he'd experienced before, and to do it as a free man. Before long, however, a deep weariness came over him. He hadn't slept in over thirty hours and wanted nothing more than to find somewhere he could lie down.

As he wandered along Broadway, Frederick came face-to-face with someone else he recognized—Jake, a slave he'd known in Baltimore, who was carrying a whitewash brush and pail. Frederick greeted him, but Jake seemed nervous and on edge. He confided in Frederick that he too had escaped, but New York City was not a safe place for any runaway slave. "The city is full of Southerners at the moment, returning home from their summer vacations in the North. One of them could easily recognize you. And slave owners hire New Yorkers to look out for runaways. You and I are worth fifty dollars apiece." Jakes' voice dropped as he continued. "There's even some black New Yorkers who'll betray you into the hands of the slave catchers for just a few dollars. Don't tell anyone who you are or where you've come from. Stay away from anywhere they might be looking for runaways like us—boardinghouses, the docks, churches. You are easy prey for kidnappers. Don't trust anyone!" With that Jake turned and disappeared into the crowd.

It would be nightfall in a few hours. Frederick had nowhere to go, and he had to avoid anyplace that might be obvious to slave hunters. He was a twenty-year-old lone black man in a city of three hundred thousand people. He was running out of money, without a job, friends, and food. *Yes,* he mused, *he was free—but free to do what?*

Chapter 9

He'd Achieved All He Set Out to Do

Unsure as to what else to do, Frederick made his way back to a familiar setting—the docks. There in the corner of a shipyard he found room behind some tar barrels to place his bags and lie down to sleep. He awoke early the next morning hungry and afraid. He got up and headed back toward Broadway and spent most of the day wandering around lower Manhattan. As he walked, Frederick constantly checked behind him to make sure no one was following. He was anxious about what he would do when his last few pennies ran out. By late afternoon he felt defeated. He stood in the street looking around. He noticed a black man open the door of a house on the opposite side of the street and walk over to him. "I've been watching you from my window," the man said as Frederick approached. "Are you in need of aid?"

Visions of betrayal and being transported south flashed through Frederick's mind as the man spoke. But Frederick knew he needed to trust someone, and the person in front of him looked honest. Frederick took a deep breath and poured out his story. The man nodded sympathetically as Frederick spoke. After Frederick described his predicament, the man introduced himself. "I'm Stewart," he said and then took Frederick's arm and guided him forward. "You'd better come inside. You can dine with us and spend the night. Tomorrow I will take you to Mr. Ruggles. I believe he's the man you need to see."

With that Frederick walked into the house. A young woman greeted him and invited him to sit at the table, where she'd added an extra plate. Frederick tried to eat slowly and politely, though he really wanted to gobble up the food as fast as he could to calm his growling stomach. It was well past dinner before he began to relax. By now he was almost certain that Stewart meant him no harm and that Mr. Ruggles was indeed the man he needed to meet.

After the best night's sleep Frederick had had in weeks, he and Stewart walked a few blocks to the corner of Lispenard and Church Street, where a tall redbrick building stood with a sign in the window that read, "Welcome to the Abolitionist Reading Room." A bell jingled as they walked in the door. "Ah, Mr. Ruggles, I have brought you a new customer," Stewart said. "I will leave him to tell you his story."

Frederick shook hands with David Ruggles, a short man with a light brown complexion like Frederick and wearing thick spectacles. "It sounds like we might be better off to talk in the back room," he said. "Come this way."

Frederick walked past rows of books as he followed David into the back room. David was a sympathetic listener and, once Frederick had finished telling him his tale, told him his own story. David was twenty-eight years old and was born to free parents in Connecticut. At age sixteen, he had settled in New York City after being a sailor for several years. Since then, he told Frederick, he'd dedicated himself to helping black people in the city in any way he could.

Frederick had assumed that because New York was a Northern state, it stood staunchly against slavery, but David echoed what Jake had told him on the street two days before. New York may be in the North, but its wealth came from Southern cotton plantations, and that was where the loyalty of the state's rich and powerful men in banking, insurance, shipping, and manufacturing lay. David explained that the economy of New York City depended heavily on Southern cotton and that half of all imports and exports into and out of the United States passed through the city. Point by point, David laid out for Frederick the ways in which white society in New York pushed down black people. While white men in New York had the right to vote regardless of whether they had money, black men had to prove they owned $250 worth of property in order to claim their voting privilege. Not only that, but they also had to be a resident in the state far longer than white men.

And although slavery had been outlawed in New York State in 1827, Southern people were welcome to come to New York with their enslaved servants and legally keep them for up to nine months. At the end of that time, all they had to do was take their enslaved servants across the state border and then return with them in order to be able to keep then as slaves in New York for another nine months. Worse yet, David told Frederick of the alarming rise in kidnappings of black people in the city. Southern agents and bounty hunters roamed the streets looking for runaways. They were aided in this by city officials who turned a blind eye as black men, women, and children were abducted and quickly shipped south. State law entitled these abducted people to a jury trial to ensure they were the legal property of someone else, but federal judges, city officials, and police officers all found ways around the law. David called the powerful men who allowed this to happen the kidnapping club. Once Southern agents and bounty hunters had established this system, it was only a small step from there to lure and kidnap free black people, especially children, and whisk them south, never to be seen by their family again. At least one child a week, and usually more, would disappear from the city, some snatched from classrooms and others off the street in broad daylight.

David explained that to respond to this situation, he had to set up the New York Committee of Vigilance three years ago. Its aim was to help freed slaves secretly move through New York and to protect unoffending, defenseless, and endangered persons of color by securing their legal rights.

David also told Frederick that he was the editor and publisher of the *Mirror of Liberty*, a magazine that reported on the vigilance committee's work. This included the volunteer effort of hundreds of brave black New Yorkers, men, women, and children. The volunteers, a vital part of the Committee for Vigilance, formed a network of spies throughout the city to alert David and other abolitionists about kidnapping activity and to hide runaway slaves such as Frederick.

Black residents of New York City also lived with all kinds of stress. Over thirty thousand people from Ireland poured into the city each year. It was the same situation Frederick had witnessed firsthand in Baltimore, only on a larger scale. The Irish immigrants, as with most of the black residents of New York City, had little education, and the members of the two groups competed for the same jobs as servants, laundresses, seamstresses, waiters, dockworkers, and laborers. David explained that over the past ten years, powerful labor unions had grown with the purpose of keeping black workers out of jobs and promoting segregation. This was evident everywhere from streetcars and steamboats to boardinghouses and restaurants.

Later that day, Frederick wrote to Anna, telling her he had arrived safely in New York City. He gave her David's address and urged her to join him there as soon as possible so they could marry and begin their future together. Since Anna couldn't read, he sent the letter, along with Antoine Stanley's Sailor's Protection Paper, to Isaac Rolles, who'd promised to read the letter aloud to Anna and return the Sailor's Protection Paper to the rightful owner. Now all Frederick could do was wait and see if Anna had the courage to join him. He felt confident she would, even though she would be leaving behind everything and everyone she knew.

David Ruggles invited Frederick to stay at his house. During the next week, Frederick met many people, black and white, who had joined forces with David to fight racism. It was dangerous to even be seen working together. During this time, Frederick read old newspaper accounts of an attempt to hold an interracial meeting in the Chatham Street Chapel five years before. The attempt brought together five thousand white people who formed a mob and rioted for three days. During that time, they controlled swathes of the city and attacked black and white abolitionists, burned down churches, and ransacked black neighborhoods.

As he read more articles in the *Mirror of Liberty*, Frederick was impressed with David Ruggles, a man who seemed to know everything and everyone who could help the antislavery cause. He went down to the docks to pull slaves out of ships' holds and smuggle them out of the city. He confronted wealthy Southerners on the streets of New York City as they walked with their slaves. He wrote articles, attended trials, and railed against the gag order on the U.S. Congress. Frederick learned that the First Amendment to the United States Constitution guaranteed its citizens the right "to petition the government for a redress of grievances." In 1834, the American Anti-Slavery Society began an antislavery petition drive. Two years later, members of the U.S. House of Representatives grew tired of listening to citizen petitions asking for the abolition of slavery in Washington, D.C. In 1836, a group of representatives from Southern and Northern states passed a resolution forbidding petitions having to do with ending slavery being read in the House of Representatives. Former U.S. president John Quincy Adams of Massachusetts was one of the few representatives to publicly stand with the abolitionists and their right to petition their government.

On September 12, 1838, a week after Frederick's arrival in New York City, Anna stood at the door of David Ruggles' home. She looked exhausted but triumphant, having followed Frederick's journey by train and ferry to be with him. Frederick was relieved to see her.

Three days later, on Saturday, September 15, Frederick and Anna were married in the parlor of David's home. The pastor who performed the small wedding ceremony was another escaped slave who had also been born on Maryland's Eastern Shore. The Reverend James Pennington had escaped Maryland at nineteen years of age, after which Quakers in Pennsylvania had taught him to read and write. As with Frederick, James loved to learn and had gone on to teach himself Latin and Greek before winning the right to sit at the back in divinity classes at Yale University. He was, however, forbidden from actively joining in class discussions or receiving a degree.

After the wedding ceremony, as they all sat down together for dinner, Frederick looked around. He'd achieved all he had set out to do. He had escaped slavery and made it to New York City, where Anna had joined him and was now his wife. It was a lot for a twenty-year-old to take in. After having come this far, he wasn't sure what to do next.

David suggested that the newlyweds travel farther north to New Bedford, Massachusetts. As the whaling capital of the world, New Bedford would have work for an experienced caulker such as Frederick. Moreover, the town had a strong community of free blacks and runaways as well as a large Quaker presence.

David gave Frederick and Anna five dollars as a wedding gift and said it would be enough to get them to the whaling port. David also had contacts there who would take them in until Frederick and Anna could establish their own home.

Frederick accepted David's advice and following the noon meal the next day, he and Anna packed their few belongings and set out for the wharves. Frederick had safely tucked their marriage certificate, the first legal paperwork he'd ever owned, into his front pocket.

The trip involved taking a steamer from New York to Newport, Rhode Island, and then traveling by stagecoach up the coast to New Bedford. By the time Frederick and Anna arrived, they'd spent their money on food and transportation. In New Bedford they were directed to the home of Nathan and Polly Johnson. The house, to Frederick's surprise, was three stories high and grander than any house the Auld family had ever lived in. Nathan and Polly, who were black, welcomed the weary travelers into their home and hearts. Frederick and Anna were shown to a third-floor bedroom from which they could see the tall-masted schooners at anchor in the harbor just a few blocks away.

Chapter 10

What He Had Been Born to Do

After a good night's sleep, Frederick was eager to learn all he could about their new hometown. At breakfast, Nathan Johnson explained how Quakers, who had little tolerance for enslaved labor, had developed the whaling industry in the United States. Conditions on whaling ships, however, were grueling, and a vessel could be away at sea for up to four years at a time, sometimes sailing as far as the Arctic or New Zealand in the Southern Hemisphere in search of whales. The pay was meager, and many sailors died from accidents and illness. Because of this, whaling-ship owners welcomed aboard and protected anyone willing to sign on to their crew, including Native Americans, black men, and runaway slaves.

The idea of being a crew member on a whaling ship and away from land for so long didn't appeal to Frederick, though he was grateful to know he'd come to a place where no slave hunter dared show his face. Nonetheless, Nathan urged Frederick to consider adopting a new last name. Doing so would remove him further from his previous circumstances, making it harder for someone to associate him with Frederick Bailey, the runaway slave from Baltimore. Frederick asked Nathan to suggest an alternative last name. Nathan pulled a book by Sir Walter Scott from the shelf. "I've been mightily impressed by this book," he told Frederick. "It's called *The Lady of the Lake.* It's an epic poem, and in it there is a Scottish clan called Douglas. Does that sound like a fitting name for you?"

Frederick took a pen, dipped it in ink and wrote on a nearby sheet of paper *Frederick Douglass and Anna Douglass* several times. He added an extra *s* at the end of the name to make it more distinctive. "Frederick Douglass, at your service," he said with a smile.

After breakfast, Frederick left Anna to help Polly bake ginger cookies while he walked down Seventh Street to Union Street. For the first time in his life Frederick wasn't afraid. He walked with his head held high, eyes straight ahead. No one was going to sneak up from behind and grab him. Frederick was confident that if he stayed in New Bedford he could be master of his own fate. It was a wonderful feeling.

Halfway along Union Street he saw a pile of coal dumped on the side of the street in front of a house waiting to be shoveled into the coal cellar. This was something Frederick could do. He knocked on the door, introduced himself to the owner, Mrs. Peabody, and asked if he could shovel her coal. Mrs. Peabody agreed, and Frederick set to work. Two hours later, he was done, and Mrs. Peabody handed him two silver half-dollars for his work.

Frederick held the coins tightly in his hand and walked toward the docks. He was already a dollar richer than when he'd arrived the night before. It was hard to believe the fact that no master was waiting for him to turn over the money. It was his, he'd earned it, and he could spend it however he wished. The sun shone a little brighter as he walked on. Frederick's heart swelled with possibilities. The two coins clenched in his hand were proof he was indeed free at last.

A week later, Frederick was feeling less jubilant. He'd gone to several shipyards seeking work as a caulker and each time was turned away. The Quaker owners of the shipyards looked at him sympathetically and explained that their white caulkers refused to work alongside black caulkers. Frederick was disappointed. Life in New Bedford was not quite as idyllic as had been described. Yet he wasn't deterred. He might not be able to earn two dollars a day as a skilled worker, but he could still earn a dollar a day as a laborer. And that is what he did.

Over the next several months, Frederick worked wherever he could. New Bedford port was home to 170 whaling ships that needed repairs and provisioning. There were other industries in town that used the whale products the ships brought back as well. In fact, New Bedford was dubbed "the town that lights America." Each year nearly two hundred thousand barrels of sperm oil, or spermaceti, drained from a cavity inside the head of sperm whales, was turned into candles in the town's seventeen candle-making factories. In addition, whale oil obtained from boiling down whale blubber aboard ships was used in various factories as an ingredient in soap, lamp oil, and lubricants for machinery and pocket watches. Also, the flexible cartilage lining the jaws of baleen whales was used to shape women's clothes, parasols, and buggy whips. Occasionally a grey chunk of fat was found in a male sperm whale's stomach. The fat, known as ambergris, was very valuable and mostly used for making expensive perfumes.

Frederick continued to find work around New Bedford. He rolled casks of oil on and off ships, sawed wood on the docks, carted coal to a candle factory, and worked the bellows of a forge at a brass foundry. It was honest work, and Frederick was proud of it. From his labor he earned enough money to move with Anna into rented rooms at 157 Elm Street. The two of them also began attending the local African Methodist Episcopal Zion Church, a small congregation made up of free and runaway black people. Before long Frederick was supervising the church's Sunday school, singing in the choir, and preaching sermons.

In January, Anna announced she was expecting a baby in the summer. This meant that money would be tighter for them, but Frederick didn't mind. He was overwhelmed that unlike everyone else in his family, he and Anna would be able to raise their own baby. They belonged together. They were a family that no master or owner had the right to tear apart.

The following month, Frederick met a man on a New Bedford street who was selling weekly subscriptions to *The Liberator*, an antislavery newspaper edited by a man named William Lloyd Garrison. Frederick told the man that he couldn't afford a subscription, but the salesman signed him up anyway—free of charge.

Frederick took his first issue of *The Liberator* home and read it through from the first page to the last. He felt his ire rise as he read an article about Catholic missionaries in Maryland who had sold south all their 272 slaves—men, women, and young children—who had worked on their six plantations. The proceeds from the sale were put toward funding the new Georgetown College in Washington, D.C. Frederick thought about how members of his own family had been sold south from Maryland, never to be seen or heard from again. Another article in the newspaper reported on the second Anti-Slavery Convention of American Women that took place at Pennsylvania Hall in Philadelphia. During the convention, proslavery mobs threw rocks through the windows of the hall and then set the hall on fire, burning it to the ground.

The Liberator gripped Frederick's imagination. He was overjoyed when two months later he learned that William Lloyd Garrison was coming to New Bedford to speak at an abolitionist meeting. Frederick knew that he had to attend the meeting. He sat in the back of the room. William Garrison was a thirty-three-year-old white man, which surprised Frederick, but the man's rhetoric was riveting. Garrison was every bit as scathing in person as he was in the articles he wrote in *The Liberator.* His address was filled with condemnation of those white men and women who called themselves Christians yet supported keeping others in chains. Nothing Frederick had ever seen or heard before had inspired him as much as William Lloyd Garrison's speech.

On Monday, June 24, 1839, Anna Douglass gave birth to a daughter. As Frederick held Rosetta in his arms for the first time, he recalled the lifelong ache in his heart to know who his own father was. He thought of the babies born into the Bailey family who had been sold south as had his sister Sarah's newborn son, Henry. He also thought of Grandma Betsy raising him, his siblings, and their cousins until they were six years old and ready to be distributed by their "owner" to spend the rest of their lives enslaved. But Rosetta had a different future ahead—a free future. Frederick longed for the black parents of every newborn to be able to look forward to raising their child to adulthood as he was now able to do.

When he registered Rosetta's birth, Frederick was reminded that he didn't know his own birthday. Slave mothers had nowhere to record the date, and slave owners typically recorded only the year of a baby's birth. Anna pressed Frederick to name a date for his birthday so they could celebrate it. He thought back over the few shadowy memories he had of his mother. He'd been about seven years old when he last saw her. She had brought him a heart-shaped ginger cake and called him her valentine. Was it possible that he'd been born on or around Valentine's Day? Was that the reason she made the supreme effort to come and visit him? Frederick thought it plausible and so decided to declare Valentine's Day—February 14—his birthday. Now all three members of the Douglass family had a day of their own on which to celebrate their birthday.

The year passed quickly, with Frederick working days and sometimes nights as well. Through his effort he made enough money to provide for Anna and Rosetta. In his spare time he helped run the church, read each new issue of *The Liberator* from front to back, and attended every antislavery meeting held in New Bedford.

Before long another baby was on the way. Lewis Douglass was born October 9, 1840. The two rooms the Douglass family rented became more crowded, but Frederick and Anna were happy.

In spring 1841, Frederick was asked to speak at an antislavery meeting and describe his experiences as a slave. Following the meeting, William Coffin, a Nantucket banker, stepped forward and introduced himself. He invited Frederick to visit Nantucket in August as a guest at the island's first antislavery convention. Frederick discussed the invitation with Anna, and together they decided to leave the children with friends and attend the conference. Frederick thought about the last time he'd had any kind of real holiday. It was the ill-fated trip to the camp meeting north of Baltimore with friends. That was three years ago, and much had happened in his and Anna's lives since then. He knew they both needed a break.

On Wednesday, August 11, 1841, Frederick and Anna arrived on Nantucket Island aboard the steamer *Telegraph* and headed to the Nantucket Atheneum, where the antislavery convention, hosted by the Massachusetts Anti-Slavery Society, was being held. The convention turned out to be the largest antislavery gathering held in the United States to date. More than five hundred people, both black and white, showed up for it from all over New England and New York. Many great abolitionist orators, including William Lloyd Garrison, were there, and Frederick enjoyed listening to their impassioned speeches against the evils of slavery.

On Thursday night, after a day of hearing several thoughtful addresses, William Coffin urged Frederick to speak to the conference attendees. Frederick looked around the crowd. Hundreds of people were present, and speaking to them seemed daunting. Yes, Frederick had preached many times before at the AME Zion Church, but always to black people. Most of those attending the antislavery conference, however, were white. Nonetheless, it was an important moment, and Frederick knew that he should accept the challenge.

A boost of courage surged through him as he stood to speak. But as Frederick approached the podium, his courage left him. His hands shook nervously, and he tried to steady them by firmly holding the edge of the podium as he greeted the crowd and began his talk. It wasn't long before his nervousness evaporated. Frederick spoke confidently about his time in bondage as a slave. He described what it was like to be beaten by Edward Covey, to be forbidden to read by Hugh Auld, and to watch his family paraded and divided, some even sold to the highest bidder when Captain Anthony died. Those in the hall sat spellbound listening to him.

When Frederick had finished speaking, William Garrison leapt to his feet and ran to the podium. "Have we been listening to a thing, a piece of property, or a man?" he yelled.

"A man! A man!" the crowd roared back.

"Shall such a man be held a slave in a Christian land?" William asked.

"No! No!" came the reply.

"Shall such a man ever be sent back to bondage from the free soil of old Massachusetts?"

With a tremendous roar, those gathered sprang to their feet and continued shouting, "No! No! No!"

William put his arm around Frederick's shoulders as the two men stood side by side. The audience surged forward and surrounded them.

The following morning, William asked Frederick to be an agent for the Massachusetts Anti-Slavery Society. Frederick could tell his own stories and urge everyone—black and white—to rise up and defeat slavery in the United States. Frederick's heart soared as he listened to William's request. This, he knew, was what he had been born to do. He was also in awe of and honored to think that William Lloyd

Garrison thought highly enough of him to offer him the position. He supported William's views on how and when to end slavery and gladly accepted the position of agent.

Frederick was then introduced to John Collins, a white man ten years his senior, with a reputation as an effective organizer. John explained that the two of them would travel from town to town riding by train or carriage or walking, if necessary. They would stay in the homes of fellow abolitionists and talk to large and small gatherings in churches, courthouses, parks, and anywhere else they could find a group of people who would listen to their message.

Within a week of returning to New Bedford, Frederick was ready to begin his new career as an agent for the Massachusetts Anti-Slavery Society. He was aware that the role had its challenges, not just from outside the abolitionist movement but from within. He quickly learned that abolitionists held differing opinions as to how to bring an end to slavery in the United States but also that people could be very passionate about their position. As far as Frederick could understand from discussions with other abolitionists and reading various antislavery pamphlets and newspapers, there were four main opinions that united or divided abolitionists.

The first of these opinions was immediatism, which focused on the idea that all slavery should end right now, that not another day should pass in the United States with people living in bondage. This view allowed no room for gradual emancipation. Slavery was a national sin that must be rooted out immediately. William Garrison believed firmly in this position.

The second opinion revolved around whether the use of violence to end slavery was justified. Some people argued that slavery was violent toward the slaves, many of whom were ill-treated by and sometimes died at the hands of their owners. They believed that if slave owners were killed in freeing them, the price was worth paying. Others, such as the Quakers and William Garrison, preferred non-violence. They argued that there was a peaceful way to free slaves and that it was their job to convince white Southerners and their Northern sympathizers to change their minds.

The next opinion had to do with the role of Christian ministers and churches in keeping slavery in place. Frederick thought back to the Methodist church the Aulds attended in Baltimore. The church minister argued that slavery was part of God's plan and that slaves had a religious duty to obey their owners and do what they told them to do. The Catholic church in Maryland had been involved in selling south enslaved children—some as young as two years old—whom they owned. And then there were those, such as William Garrison, who railed against white churches in the North as well as in the South for their role in enabling slavery to continue. Because of this, many church ministers refused to let William Garrison speak to their congregations.

The final opinion dividing abolitionists had to do with the ultimate goal of abolition. Was it enough to end slavery in Southern states, or did it involve fighting for the rights of all black people—the right to vote or the right to sit anywhere on public transportation? Was the final goal of abolition to entitle any black person to legally do anything a white person could do in the United States? William Garrison often wrote about the rights of black people and their need to be treated equally with white people. Just as radically, he believed that women should have the same legal rights as men.

Frederick's first public speaking circuit as a Massachusetts Anti-Slavery Society agent covered three states: Massachusetts, New Hampshire, and Rhode Island. Frederick and John Collins stayed in the homes of fellow abolitionists and spoke most afternoons and evenings. Sometimes the crowd that turned out to hear them numbered in the hundreds. Other times just a few people gathered. Frederick traveled with his copy of *The Columbian Orator*, which he often read for hints on how to speak better in public. In some cities Frederick got to be part of large abolitionist rallies where he spoke alongside Wendell Phillips, Stephen Foster, and the fiery Quaker woman, Abby Kelly. At first Frederick was starstruck by this. He was much younger than all of them and much less educated, but he soon realized he had something none of them had—experience. No amount of talking about slavery could replace the firsthand experience of someone who had been born and raised as a slave and whose body bore brutal scars to prove it.

Frederick and John discovered that it wasn't always easy for a white man and a black man to travel together. This was especially true when they traveled by train and sat together. Before long a conductor would come by and demand that Frederick move to the Negro car where blacks were expected to sit while riding the train. To such an indignity Frederick always responded in the same manner. He would look the conductor in the eye and say to him, "If you will give me any good reason why I should leave this car, I will go willingly; but without such reason, I do not feel at liberty to leave. Though you can do with me as you please, I shall not resist." Then John would come to Frederick's defense, trying to reason with the conductor. Sometimes the conductor wouldn't know what to do. Frederick's height and solid build made him a formidable challenge to physically remove him from his seat and send him to the Negro car.

On two occasions the conductor became incensed with Frederick and returned with a group of thugs employed by the railroad company to enforce its rules. While Frederick and John would not fight back, neither would they cooperate. Instead they sat together resolutely with their arms linked, making it difficult for the enforcers to eject them from the train. On one occasion they gripped the seat so tightly and would not let go that the bolts holding the seat to the floor broke free. The two men were carried away still sitting in their seats and cast off the train, their luggage following them. Undeterred, they would carry on with their journey by some other means and with another story to tell at their next meeting about the lack of dignity and the injustice black men and women constantly faced.

After five months as an agent for the Massachusetts Anti-Slavery Society and just before Christmas 1841, Frederick decided to move his family north to Lynn, Massachusetts. Lynn, a Quaker town ten miles from Boston, was a much larger hub of abolitionist activities. William Garrison helped Frederick buy timber and other supplies with which Frederick built a simple cottage on Union Street for his growing family.

Three years and three months had passed since Frederick and Anna were married in New York City. Frederick marveled at how many things had changed in their lives since then. They now had their own home, two children, and a third child on the way. Best of all, Frederick had found his calling as an abolitionist. It was dangerous but important work, and he was determined to dedicate himself to the cause until all people in the United States, regardless of the color of their skin, were free.

Chapter 11

Not Treated as a Color, But as a Man

For the next two and a half years, Frederick's entire life was occupied with the antislavery cause. In 1843, he took part in the One Hundred Conventions tour, during which a group of prominent abolitionists, both black and white, crisscrossed five northern states: New York, Pennsylvania, Indiana, Ohio, and Vermont. The aim of the tour was to deliver the antislavery message to half a million people. Those involved in the tour made speeches and gave sermons in which they cajoled, argued, and challenged their audiences to work toward a United States where, as the Declaration of Independence declared, "We hold these truths to be self-evident, that all men are created equal, that they are endowed by their Creator with certain unalienable Rights, that among these are Life, Liberty and the pursuit of Happiness."

During these exhilarating, eye-opening days for Frederick, he teamed up with many people he never dreamed of meeting when he was a slave. Dr. James McCune Smith, five years his senior, had been denied access to medical school in the United States and instead had attended Glasgow University in Scotland where he became the first black American to earn a medical degree. He returned to live in New York City and established a thriving private medical practice and volunteered his services as a doctor at the Colored Orphan Asylum. This institution took in black children whose parents had died or were not able to take care of them. Before the founding of the orphan asylum, orphaned black children were housed in jails or forced to work as chimney sweeps, since other orphanages were for white children only.

Charles Lenox Remond, born to free black parents, told grim stories about being raised in Salem, Massachusetts, even though his parents were wealthy business owners there. The Remonds' Salem home was a haven for black and white abolitionists, and Frederick spent many happy days there.

Another coworker on the antislavery circuit was Abby Kelley, a white Quaker woman whose fearlessness Frederick admired. She was equally passionate about women's rights as she was about the rights of black people, which made her more of a target than even Frederick. As a man, Frederick felt he could endure being pelted with eggs and bricks, but Abby stood right alongside him in the midst of it all. At one stop she became the first woman in the United States to address a national political convention.

Then there was Henry Highland Garnet. As a nine-year-old, he escaped slavery with his family who fled to New York, where he eventually became a Presbyterian pastor. Henry was two years older than Frederick and a powerful speaker. The two first met at the 1843 National Convention of Colored Citizens in Buffalo, New York, where Henry gave a fiery speech that he ended with, "Let your motto be resistance! resistance! resistance! No oppressed people have ever secured their liberty without resistance. What kind of resistance you had better make, you must decide by the circumstances that surround you, and according to the suggestion of expediency." While Henry was passionate, Frederick disagreed with his emphasis on resistance. Instead, he urged patience. Black people, he argued on stage, should wait a little longer before resorting to violence—resistance to death, yes, but patience first!

Despite frequent disagreements as to how the abolition movement should proceed, Frederick loved working with such a wide range of people. Through his association with them, he felt he was studying in a university of sorts. Wherever they went, they stirred up strong feelings about white people's moral right to own black people. At times, Frederick and his traveling companions found themselves in dangerous situations. On one occasion at an outdoor meeting in Indiana, a mob descended upon them, climbing onto the speaker's platform where Frederick stood. Some members of the mob began smashing the platform while others attacked Frederick, shouting "Kill him!" One of the other abolitionists came to his aid and managed to extricate Frederick from the angry crowd, but not before he was beaten, bruised, and bloodied. Undeterred by the mob or the beating, the next night Frederick was back on a reconstructed speaker's platform denouncing slavery.

By the time the One Hundred Conventions tour was over, Frederick had risen to become a stirring orator. This rankled many white people who spread rumors that he was lying about his past, that he wasn't a runaway slave at all. Many critics took note of how well Frederick spoke, the way he used big words, and how he talked about constitutional and biblical rights and questioned how he could possibly be a runaway. A slave who hadn't been to school could never speak or argue the way Frederick Douglass did. Frederick could debate university graduates and hold a thousand people's attention with his words. No slave, runaway or not, had that skill, the skeptics argued. From this they decided that either Frederick was not a runaway slave; perhaps some well-educated person was propping him up and writing his speeches.

Given this, Frederick set himself a new goal. He would write a book about his life. He knew that doing so was dangerous. Once his story was in print, his enemies could and most likely would use the information he presented against him and try to have him kidnapped and returned south. Many judges and constables would have no problem using Frederick's written words to show he had "stolen" himself from Thomas Auld, his rightful owner.

Despite the risks, Frederick felt exhilarated as he gathered paper and pen and began writing his *Narrative of the Life of Frederick Douglass, an American Slave.* The book focused on his time as a slave so that readers could grasp how horrible the system of slavery was and how it affected everyone involved: the slave, the slave master, his family, and society. Frederick believed that people in the South were blinded by the system of slavery surrounding them, and he intended to use his pen to rip off their blinders.

Frederick wrote at the kitchen table in the Douglass home in Lynn, Massachusetts, surrounded by his wife and children. By now he and Anna had four children, six-year-old Rosetta and three younger sons, Lewis, Frederick, and newborn Charles Remond Douglass, whom Frederick had named after his friend and fellow abolitionist campaigner.

Sometimes the words flowed. Frederick enjoyed describing his memories of fishing in the Tuckahoe Creek with his sisters and his first shipboard experience sailing on the *Sally Lloyd* with his cousin Tom. But there were challenging physical and emotional memories as well, such as watching his family be divided; being forbidden by Hugh Auld to learn to read, whipped by Edward Covey, and beaten up at the shipyard in Baltimore; and surviving his tense and daring escape north.

Frederick wrote the last line of his book in January 1845. It was published in May that year and sold five thousand copies in the first four months, making it an instant best seller and Frederick Douglass a household name.

With the publication of *Narrative of the Life of Frederick Douglass, an American Slave,* Frederick's friends and traveling companions reminded him of what he knew very well: writing a book in which he gives his birth name, along with the name of his master and other details of his early life made him a target of slave hunters. Anna and the children were safe. They were all free, but in the eyes of white Southerners and even some Northerners, Frederick wasn't really free at all. To them he was a runaway slave and still the rightful property of his owner. After giving the situation much thought, Frederick decided it might be best for him to leave the United States, at least until the uproar caused by the publication of his book died down.

To this end Frederick chose to go on a speaking tour of the British Isles. An Irish Quaker named Richard Webb had offered to print an Irish edition of his book. To support himself, Frederick planned to sell the books in the meetings at which he spoke. He also hoped to send money back to Anna when he could, though William Garrison had assured Frederick that he would help take care of his family while he was gone.

In Boston, on Saturday, August 16, 1845, amid fanfare, Frederick stepped aboard the *Cambria,* a new 219-foot-long side-wheel steamship, for the eleven-day voyage across the Atlantic Ocean to Liverpool, England. He was traveling with James Buffum, a wealthy, white abolitionist, and the famous Hutchinson Family Singers. The four members of the family, brothers Asa, John, and Judson, and their sister Abby, were a sensation in the northern United States. No one had seen anything like them before, a musical family who wrote and sang their own songs at abolitionist rallies and conventions. They were set to tour England, and Frederick hoped to meet up with them at various points along the way, as well as with William Garrison, who was scheduled to arrive in England later in the year.

Despite the enthusiastic send-off, within hours Frederick was enveloped by a sense of doom. He remembered how often he had stood on the shore of Chesapeake Bay and envied the ships, their sails billowing as they headed out to sea. He had longed to be aboard one of them and be free. Now he found himself aboard a ship headed across the Atlantic Ocean, but the ugly tendrils of racism still tugged at him. Although the *Cambria* was a British-owned vessel and James had bought first-class tickets for the journey, Frederick, because of the color of his skin, was forced to accept a lesser cabin in steerage. He was humiliated and disheartened, though such an outcome was not entirely unexpected. Regardless, Frederick got to know his fellow passengers. Some white passengers even made their way to the forecastle deck to talk with him and listen to the Hutchinson Family Singers perform.

Also aboard the *Cambria* were slaveholders from Georgia and Cuba. As far as Frederick could tell, the slaveholders were out to pick a fight with him. He and James sold copies of *Narrative of the Life of Frederick Douglass, an American Slave*, and each day the battlelines between those with abolitionist leanings and the slaveholders grew more distinct. Ten days into the voyage, the day before the *Cambria* was due to dock in Liverpool, the ship's captain, Charles Judkins, invited Frederick to give a speech on the main deck for the passengers and crew. Frederick was only a few sentences into his address when the mood turned ugly as several of the slaveholders began to heckle and interrupt him. "That's a lie," one of them bellowed, while a Cuban slave owner shouted threateningly, "I wish I had you in Cuba." This was followed by a slaveholder from Georgia who added, "I wish I had him in Savannah! We would use him up!" With that, several men rushed toward Frederick, threatening to throw him overboard. As the situation spun out of control, Captain Judkins and several burly crew members stepped in to break up the disturbance. The captain declared that he would put members of the mob in irons if they didn't stop.

With the captain's intervention, tensions eased. But once again, Frederick, who longed for personal peace, had ended up a lightning rod for racial injustice. While he was disappointed in the outcome, he realized this kind of opposition could well work out in his favor.

Sure enough, it did. For some reason, after the *Cambria* had docked in Liverpool, the group who instigated the disturbance went straight to the press to defend their actions and justify their opposition to Frederick Douglass. When he read the subsequent article in the newspaper, Frederick chuckled to himself. The Southern slaveholders were so eager to defend their honor aboard ship that they had given him and the Hutchinson Family Singers the kind of free publicity they could have only dreamt about.

Frederick spent four days in Liverpool before boarding a ferryboat to Dublin, Ireland, where he had an appointment with Richard Webb to discuss the final details of the Irish publication of his narrative.

The meeting with Richard went well. Frederick had planned to recross the Irish Sea back to Liverpool after the meeting and begin his tour in England. But he found he couldn't leave. He'd fallen in love with Ireland, or rather with the way he felt there. He had never before been anywhere where he experienced being treated as an equal in everyday life. He wrote in his diary,

> Instead of the bright, blue sky of America, I am covered with the soft, grey fog of the Emerald Isle. I breathe, and lo! the chattel [slave] becomes a man. I gaze around in vain for one who will question my equal humanity, claim me as his slave, or offer me an insult. I employ a cab—I am seated beside white people—I reach the hotel—I enter the same door—I am shown into the same parlor—I dine at the same table—and no one is offended. . . . I find myself regarded and treated at every turn with the kindness and deference paid to white people. When I go to church, I am met by no upturned nose and scornful lip. I am not treated as a color, but as a man.

One of Frederick's idols was Irishman Daniel O'Connell, who fought for Ireland to be free from British control and for Catholics to get the vote. He also spoke out against oppression everywhere he went and created quite a commotion when he refused to shake the hand of a rich Southern American businessman after learning he was a slaveholder. While in Dublin, Frederick had the opportunity to hear Daniel speak at Conciliation Hall on September 29, 1845. Following the meeting, Frederick wrote a letter about it to William Garrison.

> Mr. O'Connell rose and delivered a speech of about an hour and a quarter long. It was a great speech, skillfully delivered, powerful in its logic, majestic in its rhetoric, biting in its sarcasm, melting in its pathos, and burning in its rebukes.
>
> Upon the subject of slavery in general and American slavery in particular, Mr. O'Connell grew warm and energetic, defending his course on this subject. He said, with an earnestness which I shall never forget, "I have been assailed for attacking the American institution, as it is called,—Negro slavery. I am not ashamed of that attack. I do not shrink from it. . . . I am the friend of liberty in every clime, class and color. My sympathy with distress is not confined within the narrow bounds of my own green island. No—it extends itself to every corner of the earth.

Frederick concluded his letter by saying, "I have heard many speakers within the past four years—speakers of the first order; but I confess, I have never heard one by whom I was more completely captivated than by Mr. O'Connell."

After four months in Ireland, Frederick took a ferryboat back to England with two thousand freshly printed copies of his book in hand to sell at lectures in church halls, meetinghouses, universities, even prisons—anywhere he could find an audience.

Within weeks of his arrival back in England, a group of people led by Ellen Richardson of Newcastle asked Frederick for permission to buy his freedom, which would allow him to return to the United States. However, many abolitionists in England likened buying someone's freedom to that of paying a ransom. Slave "owners," they argued, had no right to own a person in the first place, so how could it be legal—or moral—for them to buy a person from them? It would only serve to reinforce the whole system of slavery.

Frederick understood their argument, but they weren't men or women with a bounty on their heads. They were already free and spoke from theory, while he lived with the reality that he could be captured and sold south if he returned to the land of his birth. He was tired of feeling like a hunted animal.

Ellen was the friend of a wealthy lawyer in Boston, and soon letters were crossing back and forth across the Atlantic Ocean between them. By Christmas 1846, an agreement had been reached with Thomas Auld to buy Frederick for $711. The money was quickly raised and dispatched to Maryland. Within a month Frederick was holding his own manumission papers. For the first time in his life, he was legally free. Now he could safely go home to Anna and his family in the United States.

Chapter 12

The North Star

Right Is of No Sex—Truth Is of No Color—God Is the Father of Us All, and All We Are Brethren." After writing these words, Frederick nodded and put his pen down. *Yes, that's exactly what I mean to say,* he told himself. He stood and stretched his legs, satisfied that he had the motto for his newspaper. It was to be called *The North Star,* after the popular saying "Follow the North Star," which runaway slaves repeated as they escaped at night to freedom in the north.

On December 3, 1847, eight months after Frederick's return to the United States, the first edition of *The North Star* was published. It had taken much work and sacrifice to get to this stage, which included moving his family four hundred miles inland from Lynn, Massachusetts, to Rochester, New

York. Rochester was quickly becoming a boomtown. It was a major port on the Erie Canal and a gateway to those traveling farther west into the expanding United States.

During his stay in the British Isles, Frederick had time to reflect on aspects of abolition in the United States. As a result, he realized he no longer shared some of William Garrison's more radical beliefs, particularly his notion that the United States was proslavery to the core and that the Founding Fathers who kept slaves intended for that to continue in the new country they founded. The only way forward, in William Garrison's mind, was for the United States to be dissolved and for the Northern states to form a new union based upon equality for both races. Frederick wasn't so sure. He was beginning to understand the power of political action and wanted his newspaper to call black people to become engaged in politics instead of ignoring it. With so many things to think through and write about, Frederick decided that *The North Star* would comprise four pages and be published weekly. The first of the four pages would focus on abolitionist issues, while the other three would contain general news, interesting stories, and facts. The newspaper would be sold via a two-dollar yearly subscription.

To help him with the newspaper, Frederick recruited another black abolitionist, Martin R. Delany, as co-editor. Even with Martin's help, Frederick realized he'd underestimated the effort involved in producing a new edition each Friday. To his advantage he had no shortage of topics to write about. Issues surrounding the fight for the abolition of slavery and equal rights for black people were being debated more than ever, with a new wave of controversy boiling to the surface every few months. Many of these controversies arose because of the United States' rapid expansion. In 1818, when Frederick was born, twenty-one states made up the Union. That number had risen to twenty-seven, of which fourteen allowed slavery and thirteen did not. In the years since 1812, the U.S. Congress had worked hard to admit states into the Union in pairs—one slave state and one free state—so as not to upset the voting balance between North and South.

As 1848 began, all eyes turned westward. After a year and a half of fighting, the war between Mexico and the United States was over. In the Treaty of Guadalupe Hidalgo, Mexico ceded its northern territories west of Texas, including Alta California, to the United States. In exchange Mexico would receive fifteen million dollars from the United States. No sooner had the treaty been signed and Alta California had come under U.S. control than gold was discovered there. This, in turn, led to a speedup of the necessary steps that would admit California into the Union along with Wisconsin. But both states wanted to enter as free, not slave, states, which would upset the balance of power in the Union.

As Frederick wrote about these things in *The North Star,* he became more convinced that the way to emancipation was through political change. More than that, his new abolitionist friend John Brown had persuaded him it would be impossible to bring about that level of change without violence. Wealthy men and women of the South, he pointed out, would not give up their property and their way of life without a fight.

From the day he met John Brown at his home in Springfield, Massachusetts, Frederick had been impressed with him. John was a strong and determined man in his late forties who often quoted Patrick Henry's words that heralded the American Revolution: "Give me liberty or give me death." He had a large family that included seven adult sons, most of whom had moved to Kansas in anticipation of that territory becoming a state.

Meanwhile, in 1848, another struggle for justice and equality was taking shape in the United States, this time for the rights of women. In 1840, the first World Anti-Slavery Convention was held in London, England. Several American women attended the convention, including sixty-five-year-old Lucretia Mott, a Quaker with six children, and Elizabeth Cady Stanton, who was much younger and on her honeymoon. Even though the women had been appointed as official delegates, the men at the convention voted to pass a resolution requiring women in attendance to sit in their own section behind a curtain so they could not be seen or heard by the male abolitionists. Some men, including Charles Remond and William Lloyd Garrison, were outraged and sat with the women.

While they were a generation apart in age, Lucretia Mott and Elizabeth Cady Stanton vowed to work together to bring equal rights not only to black people but also to women. Eight years later, in 1848, the two women hosted the first Women's Rights Convention at Seneca Falls, New York. For the convention, Elizabeth Cady Stanton authored "The Declaration of Sentiments," which expanded upon the Declaration of Independence by adding the word *woman* whenever the word *man* was used. The document also listed eighteen grievances, including the right for women to divorce husbands who drank or gambled without the law making them leave their children behind with him. Another issue highlighted was equal pay for equal work, since many women could expect to earn only half of what a man earned for doing the same job. Men justified this disparity by arguing that they had to work hard to provide for their families, while a woman was merely earning money for herself. These issues were controversial, but the one that really scandalized people was the call for suffrage, the right for women to vote and elect the people who would represent them in places of power.

Unlike many other men, Frederick stood one hundred percent behind the Declaration of Sentiments. He was proud to attend the convention in Seneca Falls and was the only black person among the about three hundred people in attendance. When it looked as though the gathering might vote against pursuing the right for women to vote, Frederick leapt to his feet to argue vigorously for the motion. He won the day, and the Declaration of Sentiments became the handbook for a new movement. Frederick proudly signed his name to the document, along with sixty-eight women and thirty-two men, all of whom risked ridicule for doing so. Frederick returned from the convention to *The North Star* glad that he had lived up to the motto he'd given his newspaper, "Right is of no sex—."

Frederick and Anna were also involved with the Underground Railroad, a network of safehouses and waystations that would house fugitive slaves making their way north to freedom. The network was started by Harriet Tubman, a fellow escaped slave from Maryland's Eastern Shore whom Frederick knew and greatly admired. Rochester was situated on the southern shore of Lake Ontario, and directly north from it across the fifty-mile stretch of water was Canada. Frederick and Anna used their home in Rochester and the newspaper office to hide runaways, sometimes one at a time, sometimes entire families, as they made their way north to Canada.

On March 22, 1848, Anna gave birth, this time to another daughter whom they named Annie. They now had two daughters and three sons. Rosetta, their oldest child, was now ten years old. Frederick hoped that Annie would grow up in a United States that gave her the full rights of a citizen, even though she was black and female.

As 1850 began, such a future for Annie and the other children looked less likely to unfold. A compromise had been brokered by Senator Henry Clay that sought to defuse the rising political tensions between slave and free states over the status of territory acquired at the end of the Mexican-American War. Many Southerners were now pushing for the expansion of slavery into this new territory. This was staunchly opposed by many Northerners. Under Henry Clay's compromise, which Congress eventually agreed to, California was admitted to the Union as a free state and the western boundary of Texas was established. The remaining land acquired from Mexico was organized into New Mexico Territory and Utah Territory. The people living in each of these territories would be allowed to decide whether slavery should be permitted in them. The compromise also banned the slave trade in Washington, D.C., and included a tougher fugitive slave law.

Until this time public employees or private citizens in Northern states were not legally required to help capture or return runaway slaves to their "owners." But under the new Fugitive Slave Act of 1850, passed as part of Senator Clay's compromise, every United States citizen, even Frederick and his fellow abolitionists, was legally bound to report, detain, and help send back any black person he or she believed to be a runaway. Any private citizen who refused to do this or, worse yet, helped hide runaways could be fined $1,000 and sentenced to six months in jail. In the pages of *The North Star*, Frederick wrote scathing rebuttals of the new law, and he and Anna redoubled their efforts to help fugitive slaves escape to freedom.

During 1851, *The North Star* encountered financial difficulties. Frederick merged his newspaper with another, more financially stable abolitionist journal called the *Liberty Party Paper*. The new publication that emerged from this union was known as *Frederick Douglass' Paper*.

On July 4, 1852, in celebration of Independence Day, Frederick was invited by the Rochester Ladies' Anti-Slavery Society to give a speech at Corinthian Hall. For the speech he chose to talk about two types of Americans—those who celebrated their liberation from British tyranny and those who still experienced the tyranny of slavery every day and longed for their own Independence Day. As thirty-two-year-old Frederick Douglass stood at the front of the crowded Corinthian Hall, he looked out at the expectant faces of the audience and took a deep breath. He began his speech, which he had titled "What to the Slave Is the Fourth of July?", with some opening remarks about the United States' independence from Great Britain. Then he went directly to the heart of his message. Leaning in to his audience he said,

> Fellow-citizens, pardon me, allow me to ask, why am I called upon to speak here today? What have I, or those I represent, to do with your national independence? Are the great principles of political freedom and of natural justice, embodied in that Declaration of Independence, extended to us? and am I, therefore, called upon to bring our humble offering to the national altar, and to confess the benefits and express devout gratitude for the blessings resulting from your independence to us? ...
>
> Your high independence only reveals the immeasurable distance between us. The blessings in which you, this day, rejoice, are not enjoyed in common. The rich inheritance of

justice, liberty, prosperity and independence, bequeathed by your fathers, is shared by you, not by me. The sunlight that brought life and healing to you, has brought stripes and death to me. This Fourth of July is yours, not mine. You may rejoice, I must mourn....

What, to the American slave, is your Fourth of July? I answer: a day that reveals to him, more than all other days in the year, the gross injustice and cruelty to which he is the constant victim. To him, your celebration is a sham; your boasted liberty, an unholy license; your national greatness, swelling vanity; your sounds of rejoicing are empty and heartless; your denunciations of tyrants, brass fronted impudence; your shouts of liberty and equality, hollow mockery; your prayers and hymns, your sermons and thanksgivings, with all your religious parade, and solemnity, are, to him, mere bombast, fraud, deception, impiety, and hypocrisy—a thin veil to cover up crimes which would disgrace a nation of savages. There is not a nation on the earth guilty of practices, more shocking and bloody, than are the people of these United States, at this very hour.

Frederick finished his speech by reading a poem by William Lloyd Garrison titled "God Speed the Year of Jubilee." It was a hopeful poem that pointed to the possibility of a bright future when everyone in the United States could celebrate personal freedom. As the decade progressed, Frederick began to lose faith that this would ever happen. To appease Southerners, congressmen and senators from Northern states seemed willing to compromise on any issue related to slavery.

In May 1854, the United States Congress passed the Kansas-Nebraska Act that created the territories of Kansas and Nebraska and allowed white, male adult citizens of these territories to vote as to whether they should enter the Union as slave or free states. In doing this, the Kansas-Nebraska Act undid the Missouri Compromise of 1820 that allowed Maine to enter the Union as a free state and Missouri as a slave state. The compromise had stipulated Missouri's southern border would be at latitude 36° 30' and that any future territory entering the Union above that line of latitude would be a free state and any territories below would become slave states. The problem was that both the new Kansas and Nebraska territories were above the 36° 30' line but were being given the chance to vote on whether they wanted to be free or slave states.

Almost immediately violence began to break out in these new territories as hundreds of proslavery men poured into them to take up residence so they could vote. Kansas Territory became the political battlefield of the Union. So many raids, murders, and kidnappings were taking place as proslavery and antislavery groups struggled with each other for dominance that the territory was soon being referred to as "Bleeding Kansas."

Violent confrontations between supporters of slavery and those who supported abolition became common across the country, even inside the United States Senate chamber. In May 1856, Preston Brooks, a proslavery Democrat from South Carolina, attacked Senator Charles Sumner, an abolitionist Republican from Massachusetts, with a walking stick, shattering it in the process. The beating was bloody and left Senator Sumner seriously injured. Within days of the attack, fragments of the shattered walking stick had been turned into rings that Southern senators proudly wore on necklaces to show their approval of the brutal attack against an abolitionist senator.

Tensions continued to escalate in Kansas. In Lawrence, the "free" capital of Kansas, a county sheriff led a posse of men who destroyed the offices of two abolitionist newspapers, the *Kansas Free State* and the *Herald of Freedom*. The editors of proslavery newspapers gloated over the destruction. One of them, Dr. John H. Stringfellow of the *Squatter Sovereign*, wrote that proslavery forces "are determined to repel this Northern invasion and make Kansas a Slave State; though our rivers should be covered with the blood of their victims and the carcasses of the Abolitionists should be so numerous in the territory as to breed disease and sickness, we will not be deterred from our purpose."

Meanwhile, on May 21, 1856, nearly three hundred proslavery Border Ruffians attacked Osawatomie, Kansas, an antislavery town. Abolitionist John Brown's son Frederick was among the forty men who tried to defend their town from the attackers. The men were overwhelmed, the town was looted and burned, and Frederick Brown and a number of other abolitionists were killed in the battle.

Another proslavery man, General William Walker, a doctor, lawyer, and newspaper editor from Tennessee, acted on the idea that many Southern congressmen had been discussing regarding the creation of more slave states in the Union by annexing Central and South American countries. Frederick was dismayed when he learned that General Walker had found his way into Nicaraguan politics, where he had orchestrated a fraudulent election and declared himself the president of Nicaragua on July 12, 1856. His first act as president was to reinstate slavery in Nicaragua, quickly followed by declaring English the new national language and opening the country to proslavery immigrants from the Southern states of the United States.

The deep divisions in the country over slavery also played out in the interactions between two arms of government that were meant to be independent of each other: the Presidency and the Supreme Court. On Wednesday, March 4, 1857, James Buchanan, the newly elected president of the United States, gave his inaugural speech in which he made it clear he did not think Congress should play any role in regulating slavery. Instead, he suggested all federal territories should protect slave owners and their human "property." He also addressed the case of Dred Scott v. Sandford that was currently in the hands of the Supreme Court. The case revolved around Dred Scott, an enslaved man who had been taken to the free state of Illinois and the territory of

Minnesota for five years and then brought back to a slave state. Upon his return, Dred Scott petitioned the court in Missouri for his freedom. The State of Missouri had two laws: one that stated that any person of any color could sue for wrongful enslavement and one that said any enslaved person taken to a free territory automatically became free and could not be re-enslaved upon return to a slave state.

The newly elected president left no doubt in his speech that he expected the Supreme Court justices to rule against these Missouri laws and in favor of Dred Scott being enslaved once more. Just two days later, Chief Justice Roger Taney delivered the majority opinion in the case. The Supreme Court ruled that any person descended from Africans, whether slave or free, is not a citizen of the United States according to the U.S. Constitution. Secondly, they said the laws of Missouri were illegal and could not be used to confer freedom or citizenship upon non-white individuals. The court ruled that the Missouri Compromise of 1820, which had allowed these laws, was not empowered to do so, and the Compromise was declared illegal. This meant that Congress had no power to prevent the spread of slavery anywhere in new or existing states.

In the opinion, Chief Justice Taney went on to say that blacks "had for more than a century before been regarded as beings of an inferior order, and altogether unfit to associate with the white race, either in social or political relations; and so far inferior, that they had no rights which the white man was bound to respect; and that the negro might justly and lawfully be reduced to slavery for his benefit."

Upon hearing the Supreme Court's ruling, Frederick held his head in his hands in despair. He knew from firsthand experience that slavery had been of no benefit to him. The only people who benefited from slavery were white landowners. And given the tension in the country between proslavery and antislavery factions, he began to wonder if a war might be the only thing to put an end to slavery once and for all in the United States.

By 1859, the lines had hardened to the point where there was little room for debate about slavery. Frederick tried his best to inform and engage people in discussion, but he was beginning to lose hope. He worried about what might lie ahead for the nation.

Frederick met several times with his friend John Brown, who told him of his plan to liberate slaves and ferry them north. To do this John would lead a group consisting of his sons and other supporters to loot the federal armory at Harpers Ferry, Virginia. They would use the weapons to arm eighteen thousand slaves in the surrounding counties who would free themselves and escape via a chain of manned abolitionist camps through the Allegheny Mountains to freedom. John Brown's voice was urgent and uncompromising as he spoke of his plan. "God sees it. I have only a short time to live—only one death to die, and I will die fighting for this cause. There will be no more peace in this land until slavery is done for. I will give them something else to do than extend slave territory."

Frederick understood that this was John Brown's response to elected Southern officials who declared their belief that slavery was God given and the right of all Southern gentlemen. The United States government should not only accept slavery once and for all but also actively work to expand slavery wherever possible. Albert Brown, the United states senator from Mississippi, declared in a speech, "I want a foothold in Central America...because I want to plant slavery there.... I want Cuba...Tamaulipas, Potosi, and one or two other Mexican states; and I want them all for the same reason—for the planting or spreading of slavery...I would spread the blessings of slavery, like the religion of our Divine Master, to the uttermost ends of the earth."

The United States had become a powder keg waiting for a spark to ignite it and all-out war to begin. Frederick was one of the few people in the country with an idea of what that spark might be. On August 19, 1859, he took a detour from an exhausting speaking tour to visit Chambersburg, Pennsylvania, where John Brown had requested a secret meeting with Frederick before the attack on Harpers Ferry. Frederick listened carefully as John told him all about the preparations being made for the attack. John urged Frederick to join with him in the attack. Together they would make history and bring about freedom for slaves in the United States. While Frederick admired John Brown's dedication to freeing slaves and his willingness to pay for it with his own life if necessary, he was sure the plan was doomed. He explained to John that attacking the federal armory at Harpers Ferry was certain to focus every man and every weapon under the command of the United States government against him. While the raid might be well-intentioned, it was certain not to succeed. But John Brown would not be dissuaded. He had made his choice and was committed to that course of action. He explained to Frederick that despite the risks, he would not and could not abandon his plan.

Two days later, Frederick walked away from Chambersburg and John Brown. It was one of the hardest things he'd ever had to do. And while he admired John, he could not commit to his course of action. *Each of us must choose our own way to fight this evil,* Frederick thought grimly as he boarded a train for Rochester, certain that he would not see John Brown alive again.

Chapter 13

Plunged into Turmoil

On Monday evening, October 17, 1859, Frederick stood at the podium in Philadelphia's National Hall delivering a speech he titled "Self-Made Men." His voice filled the auditorium.

> I am certain that there is nothing good, great or desirable which man can possess in this world, that does not come by some kind of labor, physical or mental, moral or spiritual. A man, at times, gets something for nothing, but it will, in his hands, amount to nothing. What is true in the world of matter is equally true in the world of the mind. Without culture there can be no growth; without exertion, no acquisition; without friction, no polish; without labor, no knowledge, without

> action, no progress and without conflict, no victory.

He paused for a moment then added, "John Brown is a man of action. We have conflict now, but victory is coming!"

The crowd cheered. By now everyone had heard the news. The night before, John Brown and eighteen men had seized the federal armory at Harpers Ferry, Virginia. According to the latest reports from the telegraph office, the group was now held up in the town's firehouse. A rumor was also spreading that President James Buchanan had dispatched a company of U.S. Marines led by Colonel Robert E. Lee to rout the group.

Frederick waited impatiently for definitive word of what was going on at Harpers Ferry. He wished his friend victory but in his heart knew that was unlikely. As he'd warned John Brown when he visited him two months before in Chambersburg, his Harpers Ferry plan was a steel trap set to snap shut on him.

And snap shut it did. By lunchtime Wednesday, October 19, the telegraph wires buzzed with the news that Colonel Lee and his men had overrun John Brown and his followers, ten of whom had been killed. Frederick waited to learn their names. By dinnertime it was clear that John Brown's sons, Watson and Oliver, were dead. John Brown had been injured but taken alive.

Within hours of receiving this news, a breathless abolitionist worker knocked at the door of the house in which Frederick was staying. He announced,

"John Hurt, the telegraph operator, is one of us, an abolitionist. He has sent me with urgent news for you. He has received a dispatch to the sheriff ordering that you be arrested for conspiracy with John Brown."

Frederick stiffened at the news. "Does anyone else know this yet?" he asked.

The messenger shook his head. "John says he can delay the dispatch for three hours. He says you must go now, with all haste. By morning every proslavery man in Pennsylvania will be after you."

Frederick knew that the man was speaking the truth. Once again he was forced to flee or be arrested. He had to move quickly. Although many white people complained that all black people looked the same, that wasn't true of Frederick. His distinct hairstyle, height, and commanding voice, along with the countless photographs taken of him during his speaking tours and the published writings in various newspapers and magazines, made him one of the most widely recognized people in the United States. Frederick knew he could easily be picked out in a crowd.

Frederick left immediately. His escape route took him north to Clifton, Canada, where he stayed at a tavern to assess his situation. While there he wrote a letter to the leading newspaper in Rochester in which he said, "I am ever ready to write, speak, publish, organize, combine, and even conspire against slavery, when there is a reasonable hope of success." While in Clifton, he also read every newspaper he could find to learn more of John Brown's fate.

As he had predicted to Frederick, John Brown had thrown a match into a powder keg. Day after day news of the events at Harpers Ferry and the idea of a slave revolt made newspaper headlines. In the accompanying reports, Frederick's name was often linked with John Brown's. Investigators had found a trunk at John Brown's home that contained many of Frederick's letters to John. Governor Henry Wise of Virginia, the man in charge of the investigation, published the text of a letter he wrote to President Buchanan that read in part, "I am asking for your assistance in finding and arresting the person of Frederick Douglass, a negro man…charged with murder, robbery, and inciting slave insurrection."

John Brown's trial was swift. In the space of two weeks, he was found guilty of all charges against him and sentenced to death. With national hysteria running high over the events at Harpers Ferry, Frederick knew he had to be careful. How much faster might "justice" rain down on him, a black man, if he were to be caught? Once again it was time for him to cross the Atlantic Ocean.

On November 12, 1859, Frederick stood on the deck of the *Nova Scotia* as the ship steamed away from Quebec City bound for Liverpool, England. He wiped tears from his eyes as he wondered if he would ever see his homeland again.

After ten frigid days at sea, Frederick arrived in Liverpool and made his way to the home of Julia Griffith, a friend from his previous visit to the British Isles. Since that time she had married Henry Crofts, a Methodist minister and fellow abolitionist, and they warmly welcomed him. Julia quickly set about organizing a speaking tour for Frederick.

As in the United States, people in Great Britain were fixated on John Brown's attack and his ultimate fate. On December 2, 1859, John had been hanged at Charles Town, Virginia, seven miles west of Harpers Ferry. The British newspapers reported that he held his head high and marched determinedly to the gallows. Before stepping onto the platform, he handed his guard a slip of paper on which he had written, "I, John Brown, am now quite certain that the crimes of this guilty land will never be purged away but with blood."

As he traveled and spoke to large crowds around the British Isles, Frederick monitored the ongoing Senate investigation into the John Brown rebellion taking place in the United States. The investigation committee was headed by Senator James Mason of Virginia. At first, everyone on the committee seemed eager to learn the truth about who else was involved in the attack at Harpers Ferry. But as the weeks went by, the enthusiasm of the committee waned. Along with the letters from Frederick found in John Brown's wooden chest were letters from politicians and other prominent people with more clout than Frederick. With these letters in hand and the embarrassing and compromising information they contained, the Mason committee soon lost interest in delving any further into who else might have been involved. Each time a new piece of information was released, it led to a new round of publicity, new revelations of the horrors of slavery, and new opportunities for abolitionists to stir things up. The last thing proslavery folk needed was an abolitionist starting another rebellion and becoming a martyr. By March 1860, the fanfare surrounding the investigation had faded. Committee members soon found they had more important things to do and moved on, especially since a national election was just eight months away.

Frederick was in Glasgow, Scotland, when he read this welcome news. But within days he also received devastating news from the United States. His youngest daughter, Annie, had died from an unknown illness that affected her brain. She was just about to turn eleven years old. Frederick made plans to return home as quickly as possible to comfort his wife and children. By the end of April 1860, he had slipped back into the United States through Canada and quietly made his way to Rochester. For the next four months he stayed near home, doing his best to ease his family's pain and come to terms with his own loss.

By now the next general election was only six months away. It was also a presidential election year. At their recent national convention, the Republican Party had chosen Abraham Lincoln to be their presidential candidate. The Democratic Party, however, had been unable to settle on a single candidate and instead had two presidential candidates. Illinois Senator Stephen A. Douglas had the backing of Northern Democrats, while Vice President John C. Breckinridge of Kentucky was the Southern Democrat's candidate of choice. There was also a fourth presidential candidate in the race, former Tennessee senator John Bell, who represented the Constitutional Union.

As the election approached, Frederick worked hard to educate readers of his newspaper, now known as *Frederick Douglass' Monthly*, about their choices for president. He wasn't impressed with Abraham Lincoln and said he would not vote for him, though in his editorials he conceded that Lincoln was a good man with a great deal of common sense. The problem Frederick had with Lincoln was that he valued keeping the Union together over ending slavery in the South. Lincoln believed that the South had the right to make its own laws regarding slavery, though he held that any future territories entering the Union must be free states. Slavery could not spread any farther than it already had.

As the campaigning for president unfolded, it became obvious that Lincoln had a good chance of becoming the sixteenth president of the United States, even though he didn't have the support of the majority of voters. His big advantage lay in the fact that the Democratic Party had nominated two candidates. Had they stuck together and nominated one candidate, that person would most likely win the election. Thirty-three states now formed the United States of America, and they were politically divided into three regions. One region comprised the eleven states of the deep South whose culture revolved around slaves growing cotton. For example, over half the population of South Carolina were enslaved people who formed the backbone of the cotton-producing economy. Then there were four border states, Missouri, Kentucky, Delaware, and Maryland, where slavery was legal but whose economies did not rest upon the system. These states also had large populations of free black people. In Maryland, only an eighth of the population was enslaved. In the eighteen remaining northern and western states, slavery was illegal though many of the residents of those states did not hold a unified opposition to slavery. Most wealthy Northerners had strong ties to the South and the cotton grown there using slave labor. Shipbuilders, cotton mill owners, bankers, and insurance companies were all profiting from slavery and were particularly interested in not seeing the practice end and their profits falter. As Frederick was well aware, many of these people viewed abolitionists with a mix of suspicion and contempt.

On Election Day, Tuesday, November 6, 1860, after the votes were tallied, Abraham Lincoln had won. In four months, on March 4, 1861, he would be inaugurated as the next president of the United States. Of course, a lot of people were unhappy at Lincoln's win, and Frederick knew that much could happen in the country before he was sworn in as president. Sure enough, a lot did happen. On December 20, 1860, South Carolina announced it was seceding from the Union and would no longer be part of the United States. In January 1861, five more Southern states seceded: Mississippi, Florida, Alabama, Georgia, and Louisiana. Texas followed suit on February 1. These seven Southern states called their new country the Confederate States of

America. Meanwhile, the federal government of the United States did not recognize the right of these Southern states to leave the Union and so did not acknowledge their new "country." Instead, they referred to these states as being in rebellion.

The Confederate states elected Jefferson Davis, former United States senator from Mississippi who owned over one hundred slaves, as their president. They also chose Montgomery, Alabama, as their capital and raised a new flag with seven white stars in a circle on a blue background in the top left corner.

President Buchanan refused to act either for or against the states that had left the Union. He decided to leave dealing with the situation to the next president, Abraham Lincoln.

The country plunged into turmoil, with many Northerners blaming abolitionists for stirring things up to begin with. If they had not agitated for the end of slavery, there would have been no reason to argue so viciously about states' rights. The South, they said, could have continued practicing slavery while the North continued without it. They argued that abolitionists in the North wanted to exercise moral sway over the South. Frederick pushed back against this argument by pointing out that it was the Southern slave owners who wanted control over the North. They were the ones forcing Northerners to violate their consciences by putting the Fugitive Slave Act in place that made them responsible for arresting runaway slaves. Yes, the problem was states' rights, Frederick said bluntly, but the *particular* right they wanted to fight for was the right to own slaves.

In his inauguration speech on March 4, 1861, President Abraham Lincoln made it clear that he did not think the Constitution gave the South the power to leave the Union. They were United States rebels, not citizens of a separate country. He also did not believe that the Constitution gave him or the federal government the power to demand Southern states end slavery. He told the gathered crowd,

> I have no purpose, directly or indirectly to interfere with the institution of slavery in the States where it exists.... In your hands, my dissatisfied fellow-countrymen, and not in mine, is the momentous issue of civil war. The government will not assail you.... You have no oath registered in Heaven to destroy the government while I shall have the most solemn one to preserve, protect and defend it.

Something momentous had been set in motion, but where would it end? Like everyone else, Frederick didn't know. During this time, he preached almost every Sunday afternoon at the AME Zion Church in Rochester, where he told the congregation,

> We live but today and the measureless shores of the future are wisely hid from us. And yet we read the face of the sky and may discern the signs of the times. We know that clouds and darkness, and the sound of distant thunder means rain. There is a general feeling amongst us, that the control of events has

> been taken out of our hands, that we have fallen into the mighty current of eternal principles—invisible forces, which are shaping and fashioning events as they wish, using us only as instruments to work out their own results in our national destiny.

And just what that national destiny was, was anybody's guess.

Chapter 14

Civil War

On April 12, 1861, four and a half weeks after Abraham Lincoln was sworn in as president, Confederate soldiers opened fire on the federal troops who controlled Fort Sumter in the middle of Charleston, South Carolina's harbor. Two days later, the troops defending the fort surrendered. In the wake of the attack, things moved so quickly Frederick worked almost around the clock reporting on them in *Frederick Douglass' Monthly.* On April 17, Virginia seceded from the Union, followed by Arkansas. Meanwhile, in response to the situation, President Lincoln issued a proclamation calling for seventy-five thousand volunteers to join the U.S. army for ninety days, the length of time he presumed it would take to subdue the South.

On May 5, 1861, Frederick stood among the twenty thousand people gathered to cheer eight companies of soldiers parading to the Rochester train station. The soldiers were on their way to join the 13th New York Infantry Regiment as they rallied to Lincoln's proclamation.

As Union forces mustered to confront and subdue the Confederacy, on May 20, North Carolina seceded from the Union, followed by Tennessee on June 8, bringing the number of Confederate states to eleven. The Confederate capital was also moved from Montgomery, Alabama, to Richmond, Virginia, just one hundred miles from the federal capital of Washington, D.C. Meanwhile Maryland, Delaware, Missouri, and Kentucky, states where slavery was legal, remained in the Union, though some men from them enlisted in the Confederate army.

As Union forces gathered, Frederick wasn't so sure the Confederate states would be subdued in ninety days. Yes, the North had many strategic advantages. Almost all manufacturing, from ironworks to shipyards, was in the Northern states. The North also had a better railway system and controlled the United States navy. As for manpower, twenty-two million people lived in Union states while only nine million lived in Confederate States, and four million of those were slaves. Northerners outnumbered white Southerners four to one.

On paper, it looked like a simple war to win, but Frederick knew that many Northerners were not accounting for the fact that white people in the South were fighting for something that was deeply personal.

The practice of slavery in these states reached back nearly 250 years and spanned ten generations. As a result, many white Southerners saw slave owning as their rightful heritage. Their way of life depended upon it. To them, their slaves represented a large financial "investment." The average cost to buy a slave was eight hundred dollars, which meant that combined, the slaves in the South were worth over three billion dollars. Thus, the right of Southern states and Southerners to make their own laws regarding slavery was crucial to saving their way of life. If they lost the war and were pulled back into the Union, their way of life would completely change. The huge plantation houses, the workers in the cotton fields, the cotton merchants, and those who transported cotton would be gone. Also swept away would be the livelihoods of the thousands of poor white people who existed on the sordid edges of slavery as slave traders, overseers, those tracking and returning runaways, those who participated in mounted patrols that ensured that no black person traveled at night or were off their plantation without a pass. All the things that held four million men, women, and children in bondage.

By contrast, Frederick observed that many Northern whites were fine with the way things were. A slave picking cotton on a Mississippi plantation seemed a long way away from them. They didn't really want to think about the terrible things masters and overseers were doing to those who were enslaved. Frederick was sure that the battle ahead would be a long one. Southerners were fighting for their way of life, while many Northerners, hoping to maintain the nation's eighty-five-year-old union, seemed to Frederick too willing to make compromises.

During this time *Frederick Douglass' Monthly* was more important than ever. The looming Civil War was the catalyst abolitionists had been waiting for. They reasoned that surely now American citizens living in the North would shake off their lethargy and smash the "slave power" of those living in the South. At least Frederick hoped that would be the outcome, yet he worried that the antislavery momentum would collapse. This was likely if President Lincoln and his government compromised with Southern states and allowed them to keep slavery in exchange for returning to the Union. Frederick saw his mission as doing everything he could to keep the North focused on the issue of slavery. Every lecture he gave and every editorial he wrote hammered at the moral right of slaves to be free.

But that wasn't all. Frederick also wanted another right for Northern blacks—the right to fight. When fighting broke out at Fort Sumter, it set off a rush of free black men wanting to enlist in U.S. military units. But they were turned away. Frederick, though, was certain they should be permitted to fight alongside white men for their country and for a more equal and just future. He said, "Liberty won by white men would lose half its luster," and "Once the black man [is allowed to] get upon his person the brass letters *U.S.* and an eagle on his button and a musket on his shoulder and bullets in his pocket, there is no power on earth that can deny he has earned the right to citizenship."

Frederick longed to see his two older sons, twenty-year-old Lewis and nineteen-year-old Frederick Jr., don the Union army uniform and take up arms, but Lincoln and the War Department weren't interested in recruiting black soldiers. Putting weapons in the hands of black men and allowing them to shoot white Southern soldiers seemed unimaginable to many people living in border states such as Maryland, Kentucky, and Missouri. If black men were allowed to enlist, these states threatened to leave the Union and join the Confederacy.

On July 21, 1861, Union soldiers marched to confront the Confederate army in the first major battle of the Civil War. Confederate soldiers were marching toward Washington, D.C., and the Union army engaged them in battle along the banks of Bull Run Creek, thirty miles southwest. Things did not go well for the undertrained Union soldiers. Confederate reinforcements arrived, forcing the Union army to retreat to Washington, D.C. And after the battle, Frederick was infuriated when he learned that any fugitive slaves who made it through the Union lines were returned to the Confederates. To the political leaders in Washington, the war was not yet about slavery, though it would be soon if Frederick had his way.

Meanwhile, many people were concerned about what might happen if all the enslaved people in the South were freed at once. Would things become chaotic? Would these people take the jobs of white people? Would they kill their old masters? Opinions about what might happen were endless. Some black leaders, among them Martin Delany, who had been Frederick's co-editor when he founded *The North Star*, argued that the United States government should pay for former slaves to be relocated to Liberia, West Africa, the British West Indies, or somewhere in South America, where they could begin new lives. Lincoln also thought this a good idea, but not Frederick, who thought it insulting. His ancestors had been brought to the United States over a hundred years before, and he argued that he had as much right to stay and thrive in the U.S. as anyone else. And in his opinion, so did every slave in the South. Their labor produced enough cotton to supply three-quarters of the world's demand and in the process made the United States a wealthy country. In his newspaper editorials he asked why should black men and women be shut out of the new society that was being formed on the backs of their labor?

As the Civil War dragged on into a second year, Frederick became angry with Lincoln, accusing him of a "stand still, do nothing policy." He wanted action.

In April 1862, Union forces defeated their Confederate counterparts and pushed their way into the Mississippi River Valley. And in September, the Union won another victory at the Battle of Antietam, where over twenty-two thousand men were killed.

Following the victory at Antietam, President Lincoln issued an executive order known as the Emancipation Proclamation. The order stated that unless the Confederacy returned to the Union three months hence on New Year's Day 1863, the federal government of the United States would declare all enslaved men, women, and children in Confederate states to be free. The proclamation didn't include slaves in the border states of Missouri, Kentucky, Maryland, and Delaware that had remained loyal to the Union. Despite this, the Emancipation Proclamation reenergized Frederick and many other abolitionists. It was vital he did all he could to help the North win the war as quickly as possible.

The Emancipation Proclamation also authorized black men to enlist in the United States army and navy. As a result, the 54th Massachusetts Infantry Regiment was organized to officially recruit black men as soldiers. Massachusetts' governor put out a call for paid agents to help in the recruitment process. Frederick and his son Frederick Jr. were two of the first men to sign on as recruiters. Frederick used his vast network of friends and his columns in *Douglass' Monthly* to rally black troops. He was proud that two of the first regimental recruits were his sons Charles and Lewis.

In churches, meeting halls, and town squares across the North, Frederick urged crowds of young black men to enlist in the new regiment. He told them,

> The day dawns; the morning star is bright upon the horizon! The iron gate of our prison stands half open. One gallant rush from the North will fling it wide open, while four million of our brothers and sisters shall march out into liberty. The chance is now given you to end in a day the bondage of centuries, and

> to rise in one bound from social degradation to the place of common equality with all other varieties of men.

By April 1863, Frederick had crisscrossed the North recruiting and sent more than one hundred recruits off to train in Boston. They were former slaves and freemen living in the North, and some even came from as far as Canada and the West Indies.

Soon northern newspapers began reporting that the Confederate army had been instructed to capture any black person, enslaved or free, who lived in Union states and to transport him or her to Confederate states, where they would be enslaved and forced into work gangs. This led to scores of free blacks in Maryland and Pennsylvania being rounded up by Confederate soldiers and sent south into slavery. The more Frederick learned about this, the angrier he became with Union politicians who refused to admit that while the Confederates said they were all about "states' rights," what they really meant was their insistence on keeping other human beings enslaved generation after generation. This had to stop!

Six months after President Lincoln drafted the Emancipation Proclamation, the Union army had prevailed under General Ulysses S. Grant and gained control of the Mississippi River. Even so, it was hard for Frederick not to be discouraged by letters from his sons, who wrote saying that although black soldiers were promised equal pay and equal treatment with white soldiers, that hadn't happened. Black soldiers were paid seven dollars a month, while white soldiers received thirteen dollars a month.

Frederick continued his recruitment efforts even after a letter from his son Lewis reported that the men of the 54th Massachusetts Infantry Regiment were refusing their wages in protest and would continue working without pay until they got the same amount as white soldiers. No matter their leadership potential, black soldiers could not rise above the level of sergeant. Worse still, many Northern officers assumed that black soldiers would flee from a real battle, and so they were always assigned to noncombat duties such as digging toilets and burying the dead. During marches they were positioned at the rear, as far from the fighting as possible. So while black soldiers did much of the hard labor, they were seldom in the thick of the battle.

Frederick protested this situation in every way he could, calling for wage equality and the opportunity for black regiments to prove themselves on the battlefield. Then, on the evening of July 18, 1863, the men of the 54th Massachusetts Infantry Regiment, in which Lewis Douglass served as a sergeant, were ordered to lead an attack against Fort Wagner, a beachhead fortification on Morris Island, South Carolina, that guarded the southern approach to Charleston Harbor. The soldiers of the regiment led a doomed bayonet assault on the fort across a three-quarter-mile stretch of open beach. The fighting was brutal and impossible for Union soldiers to win. When the charge was over, 270 of the 600 soldiers who made up the 54th Massachusetts Infantry

Regiment had been killed. Lewis, who was on the front line of the attack, was not injured.

A month after the assault on Fort Wagner, Frederick was amazed to find himself sitting in the White House talking to President Lincoln. He was there to confer with the president about the treatment of black soldiers, particularly their lack of equal pay and their inability to rise above the rank of sergeant, and to discuss plans to move liberated slaves out of the South. At the end of their time together, Frederick left the White House with a new respect for Abraham Lincoln. He still disagreed with many of the president's policies but believed that the man had rightfully earned his nickname Honest Abe. He was convinced that President Lincoln would make sure that when the Civil War was over, the United States of America would be free from the curse of slavery.

On Christmas Eve 1863, as war still raged on, Frederick and Anna's oldest daughter, Rosetta, married Nathan Sprague, a soldier in the 54th Massachusetts Infantry Regiment. As they wed, Frederick hoped with all his heart that the war would be over before another Christmas passed. So far, all three of his sons had survived, but he worried about them constantly and now had a son-in-law to add to the burden.

In early September 1864, Atlanta, Georgia, fell to the Union army under the command of General Tecumseh Sherman. The soldiers destroyed most of the city and in November began a march from Atlanta to the east coast. Their mission was to completely disrupt the Southern economy and transportation networks by leveling everything in their path.

Meanwhile, on November 1, 1864, Maryland narrowly passed a bill abolishing slavery in the state and all the laws that propped it up. This included the law that forbade emancipated slaves from returning to the state. At last Frederick could go home. On Tuesday, November 15, he was back in Fells Point, Baltimore, walking the streets where as a boy he had run errands for Miss Sophia. He was also delighted to be reunited with his older sister, Eliza, who had come to Baltimore to visit him. The last time they had seen each other they were both still enslaved. Eliza was now forty-eight years old and still lived on Maryland's Eastern Shore with her husband, Peter. She told Frederick that Peter, who was free, had saved for many years to buy her freedom from the Aulds. Together they now had nine children and were all stuck in poverty.

The following afternoon, Frederick spoke at the Bethel AME Church at Fells Point. As he stood to speak, a thousand memories swirled within him of attending the church as a thirteen-year-old. The congregation applauded as he stepped into the pulpit. Frederick surveyed their faces and recognized some familiar ones, albeit older and more wrinkled.

The sermon Frederick delivered was hopeful and uplifting. He talked of how he used to stand on the shore of Chesapeake Bay and watch ships pass, their white sails billowing in the wind, and how envious he had been of their freedom. And now, every person in the church building was free. Frederick also turned his attention to the white people present. "Knowledge is power," he boomed, "and you have knowledge: Wealth is influence, and you have wealth. Majorities rule under our form of government, and you are the majority. Why are you haunted with the idea that to invest the colored race with equal rights is dangerous to the rights of white men?"

In the end, Frederick held the standing-room-only crowd spellbound for three hours, during which he not only challenged whites to make room for black people to flourish but also admonished newly freed black people to take their destiny into their own hands, to learn, experience, and take part in this new world in which they found themselves.

Yet the war dragged on, and another presidential election was held, which Abraham Lincoln again won with Andrew Johnson as his running mate. He'd made this choice to appease the South. Johnson was a senator from Tennessee who had remained loyal to the Union throughout the war and firmly believed that the federal government should not interfere with the rights of any state to set its own laws regarding voting and the treatment of former slaves. Johnson was also a former slave owner, a fact Frederick found hard to stomach.

Saturday, March 4, 1865, was inauguration day in Washington, D.C., and Frederick was in attendance. The day before, he had tea with Salmon Chase, the sixth chief justice of the Supreme Court, who would swear Lincoln into office for a second term. On inauguration day, Frederick observed the parade and then watched the chief justice swear in the president, after which Lincoln then gave his inaugural address. Frederick's spirit soared as he listened. The president addressed everything Frederick hoped he would and was amazed by how much power he had packed into his short speech.

Following Lincoln's second inauguration, the Civil War continued, but it seemed only a matter of time before the Confederacy would collapse. That process began on April 9, 1865, when General Robert E. Lee, overall commander of the Confederate army, surrendered the Army of Northern Virginia at the Court House in Appomattox, Virginia. Other Confederate forces across the South began to follow. As far as everyone in the North was concerned, the Union army had won the war. Frederick knew that the battle to create a just and equal country for all Americans had just begun.

Chapter 15

How Things Had Changed

At Easter 1865, Frederick returned to Rochester, New York, after a speaking tour to celebrate the end of the Civil War and the dawn of new hope for black people across the South. He was particularly happy that President Lincoln was talking about giving black men in the South the right to vote.

On Easter Saturday, April 15, however, celebration turned to mourning. Over telegraph wires and via messengers, news quickly spread that the previous night Abraham Lincoln had been shot in the head while attending a play at Ford's Theatre in Washington, D.C., and had died early Sunday morning. Frederick could hardly believe it. While he'd cycled through so many emotions during the war, nothing shook him like learning the president of the United States had been assassinated by a Southern sympathizer.

That afternoon Frederick joined the throng of people streaming into Rochester's City Hall. He stood near the back as he listened to the mayor and several prominent white clergymen address the crowd. As they spoke, many people, including Frederick, wept openly.

After a while, the men and women surrounding Frederick chanted, "Douglass! Douglass! Douglass!" and parted to make a way for him to get to the podium. Standing before the crowd, it seemed fitting to Frederick to use Lincoln's words and not his own. In a somber tone he recited the president's recent inaugural speech, which he'd witnessed six weeks before.

> With malice toward none; with charity for all; with firmness in the right, as God gives us to see the right, let us strive on to finish the work we are in; to bind up the nation's wounds; to care for him who shall have borne the battle, and for his widow, and his orphan—to do all which may achieve and cherish a just, and a lasting peace, among ourselves, and with all nations.

Frederick concluded his recitation of Lincoln's speech by adding, "Today is a day for silence and meditation, for grief and tears."

Frederick's grief and tears soon gave way to despair as Vice President Andrew Johnson was sworn in as president. Although Congress wasn't scheduled to meet until December, following the surrender on May 4 of the remaining Confederate forces in Alabama and Mississippi, Johnson moved swiftly. On May 9, 1865, he officially declared the Civil War over. He then took it upon himself to decide the conditions under which Confederate states could reenter the Union. He required them to uphold the abolition of slavery, which was enshrined in the Thirteenth Amendment to the United States Constitution that Congress had passed on January 31, 1865; swear loyalty to the Union; and pay off their war debts. In exchange, Southern states were free to make any laws they wanted restricting the rights of former slaves. And make laws they did. These became known as black codes. In Mississippi and South Carolina, black people were required to have legal contracts to show they were employed for the coming year. Plantation owners were allowed to pay them at the end of each year, and if they left their job early, they could be hunted down and arrested. Nor were they able to negotiate their pay. In South Carolina, the codes also stated that black people had to pay for a special permit to earn money in any way other than as a farmworker or servant. Young, orphaned black children were "given" to plantation owners to work for them for free. In many ways, black people in these states were just as hobbled as they had been as slaves. Once again Frederick felt his voice was needed to represent Southern blacks. He returned to the lecture circuit and plotted ways to influence the new president.

As he continued to speak out, Frederick joined forces with his old abolitionist friends to decry racism at meeting halls and conventions across the country. As they spoke, Frederick was saddened but not shocked at the level of violence and hatred that descended upon the South. Fights broke out that led to riots that were often followed by massacres and other terrible crimes. In Memphis, Tennessee, an argument over a horse-drawn carriage accident ended with forty-six black people being killed. In New Orleans, the city police, who were former Confederate soldiers, attacked a public march held by black people, many of whom were former Union soldiers. The police opened fire, and thirty-six people were killed while more than one hundred were wounded. Frederick received a steady stream of reports of black schools, businesses, and homes being burned, women being assaulted, and men hanging from trees in public spaces. To him it was proof of what he'd said all along. Abolition wasn't enough. Black people wouldn't be truly free until they had the same rights as white people, most importantly, the right to vote.

Frederick spent most of his time traveling and speaking, and when he returned home to Rochester it was to an ever-changing family scene. Oldest daughter, Rosetta, and her husband, Nathan, now had two little girls, Annie and Harriet, and lived in the family home. They watched over Anna, who had started having fainting bouts. Meanwhile, Charles had married eighteen-year-old Libby Murphy, and while Charles looked for work in Washington, D.C., Libby gave birth to their son, Charles Frederick (Freddie), at the Douglass home in Rochester. The marriage of another son quickly followed, this time

Frederick Jr., who married Virginia Hewlett. Soon they too had a son whom they named Frederick, after his father and grandfather.

During summer 1867, Frederick's brother, Perry, along with his wife, Maria, and their four children arrived unexpectedly in Rochester. Frederick was delighted to see his brother again, though the gap between them was painfully wide. Perry was old beyond his years and bent from a lifetime of picking cotton. His children had never lived in a proper house or slept in a bed with sheets. Frederick's children soon began to complain about their new cousins from the South.

The following year, Frederick found himself backed into a corner by women suffragettes. He'd always supported women getting the vote and was proud to have been the only black man to sign the Declaration of Sentiments at the Seneca Falls Women's Rights Convention in 1848. But now, twenty years later, there came a parting of ways. Women suffrage leaders Elizabeth Cady Stanton and Susan B. Anthony announced that they wouldn't support ratification of the Fifteenth Amendment, which would give black men the right to vote, unless it also included the right of women to vote. The two women called anyone, including Frederick, who might support their cause. They argued it would be better if no one got the vote rather than leave women out of the deal. Frederick was deeply disappointed in their stand, but he could not give up his support of the opportunity for black men to get the right to vote. He was confident it would pave the way for women's voting rights.

Despite the opposition of Elizabeth Cady Stanton and Susan B. Anthony, on May 19, 1870, Frederick was once again in Baltimore, this time to celebrate ratification of the Fifteenth Amendment. Black men had won the right to vote.

In August 1863, *Frederick Douglass' Monthly* had ceased publication. But now that the Fifteenth Amendment had been ratified, Frederick felt he needed a new way to voice his concerns about how many new laws were being designed and put into place in such a way as to keep Southern blacks tied to the plantations and out of schools and public debate. To amplify his concerns, he founded another newspaper, the *New National Era,* based in Washington, D.C.

Black people in the South—and in the North as well—were still in danger. Frederick found this out for himself on the evening of June 3, 1872. He was in Washington, D.C., and received a telegraph saying his home in Rochester, New York, had burned to the ground. Everyone in the house, including Rosetta's four young children, had escaped unharmed. Frederick's mind immediately went to the editorial he'd written for the *New National Era* a week before. In it he called out Southern Democrats for hiding behind the Ku Klux Klan, whose members were terrorizing Southern blacks and burning down schoolhouses and churches. And now his home was gone too. He caught the first train home to Rochester to see what could be done.

Son-in-law Nathan told Frederick that the fire had started in the barn, where no one in the family had lit a candle or a lantern since winter. From the barn the fire quickly spread to the house. Fortunately, Frederick's library was on the bottom floor of the house and several neighbors arrived in time to save his precious books. Frederick was grateful. He was also convinced that someone had deliberately lit the fire. It was a bitter blow to a man who had arrived in New York thirty-four years earlier with so little—no birth certificate, no records of his family, no money, and three books: his Bible, a copy of *The Columbian Orator*, and Webster's spelling book. Now, standing in stunned silence beside Anna, he stared at the charred remains of eleven thousand dollars in paper bonds, thousands of historically important letters and documents, copies of his newspapers, along with all the records of his family, including his marriage certificate, the first official paperwork he'd possessed. Fortunately, his beloved copy of *The Columbian Orator* had been saved.

Following the fire, Frederick decided not to rebuild the house. Instead, he moved his family to Washington, D.C., where he rented a house on A Street, just blocks from the U.S. Capitol. Soon afterward the United States was hit by an economic recession, and Frederick did his best to keep himself and his ever-expanding family afloat. The next three years proved difficult. The *New National Era* newspaper went under financially, and Charles, Frederick, Jr., and Lewis Douglass found employment whenever and wherever they could.

By early 1877, Frederick and Anna had eleven grandchildren living with them or around them in

Washington. These included Rosetta and Nathan's four daughters and a son. Their ten-year-old daughter, Alice, had died of heart failure the year before. Frederick Jr. and Virginia still had their oldest son, Freddie, who was now six years old, but their next three children all died before their first birthday. Meanwhile Charles and Mary had six children, three boys and three girls. Frederick enjoyed his grandchildren, but he was concerned about their future.

Soon after his inauguration as the nineteenth president of the United States, on March 4, 1877, Rutherford B. Hayes appointed Frederick as the United States marshal for the District of Columbia. The position required Senate approval, and Frederick was the first black man to serve in the role. His job as marshal involved helping to run the federal court in Washington. Frederick was honored to have been appointed to the position and relieved that it paid well.

Frederick was now in his sixtieth year. Over the years his mind often wandered back to his early life in Maryland. On June 17, 1877, he found himself back in St. Michaels, Maryland, where he knocked on the door of his old master. It had been forty-one years since Thomas Auld had sent Frederick back to live with his brother in Baltimore, and now Thomas had asked to see Frederick. Upon hearing the request, Frederick didn't hesitate to make the trip, though he wasn't sure how being face-to-face with the man who once held his fate in his hands would go.

Thomas was propped up in bed. He was old and feeble, but his eyes lit up when Frederick entered the bedroom. "Marshal Douglass," he declared.

"No, not Marshal, but Frederick to you, as it used to be."

His old master nodded his head slowly and wiped tears from his cheeks. "Frederick it is then, like the old days. I am glad to see you. I have followed your work. Thank you for coming to see me."

Frederick looked down at the old man, now over eighty years old and laboring to breathe. *Time is the great leveler,* he thought. *This man once had the power of life and death over me, and now he stands at the edge of eternity, pitifully grateful for a kind word from me.*

The two men talked about Thomas's first wife and how she had been so kind to Frederick as a boy. They also spoke about Thomas's decision to send Frederick to Baltimore after his failed escape attempt instead of sending him South. "I have always wondered what you thought about my running away," Frederick said.

Thomas smiled. "I always knew you were too smart to be a slave. Had I been in your place, I would have done the same thing."

"You know, I did not run away from you, but from slavery," Frederick said.

After his time with Thomas, Frederick visited his brother, Perry, whose wife, Maria, had died. Perry was in dire straits, and Frederick invited him to come to Washington to live with him. Perry packed a few belongings into a sack, and the two left right away.

Soon afterward, Frederick bought a house on a hill above the Anacostia River in Washington's first suburb. The property had a fourteen-room house, a barn, and huge vegetable and ornamental gardens, all set on nine acres of lawn. Frederick called the new place Cedar Hill, and the house soon overflowed with family members and visitors. Some stayed a week, others a year or more. Frederick had a simple stone cabin built on the property, like the one Grandma Betsy had raised him in. The cabin had a single room with a fireplace and no windows and was furnished with a desk, chair, couch, and bookshelf. Frederick called the cabin the "growlery," and he retreated there when he wanted to be alone to think or write. By now he was busy updating his autobiography.

The following year Frederick visited Maryland's Eastern Shore once more. This time he walked over the land at Tuckahoe Creek where he'd been born. There was no sign of his grandmother's cabin, but the steep bank he slid down as a four-year-old was still there, as was the muddy shoreline where he'd fished with his cousins. Lost in his thoughts, he scooped up some dirt to take back to Washington with him.

On his visit, Frederick also gave a lecture in Easton. As he was escorted into the courthouse, he glimpsed the barred windows of the old jail cell in which he'd been incarcerated after the failed escape attempt. He shook his head as he passed it. How things had changed!

In 1881, Frederick finished the new version of his autobiography *Life and Times of Frederick Douglass*. Soon afterward President James Garfield appointed him to be the Recorder of Deeds for the District of Columbia. The job entailed maintaining public records and documents, especially those relating to real estate ownership. It also entitled Frederick to government transportation. That summer he made another trip back to Maryland's Eastern Shore, this time to visit the old Wye plantation. He felt jubilant as he sat as a guest on the front porch of the Great Farmhouse. So often as a boy he'd stood at a distance in his ragged linen tunic and bare feet, imagining what it would be like to sit on the porch talking with important people. Now he was doing exactly that and being treated with dignity by white people.

Frederick arrived back at Cedar Hill to find Anna's condition getting worse. She was fainting more frequently, and before long she was bedridden. Anna died on August 4, 1882, just short of their forty-fourth wedding anniversary. She had been Frederick's anchor for forty-five years, and he mourned her death. He wondered how he would go on without her.

Chapter 16

His Words Remain an Echo

The next year proved difficult for Frederick. He missed Anna and found it hard not to dwell on the past. He continued his work as Recorder of Deeds for the District of Columbia. As he gradually began to regain his interest in the world around him, his next-door neighbor, Hiram Pitts, asked him if he could find a job for his niece, Helen, in the Recorder of Deeds office. Frederick was glad to do so. He'd known the Pitts family for many years. Helen's parents, farmers in Honeoye, New York, had been outspoken abolitionists. Frederick had stayed with them several times during early speaking tours. He remembered Helen, who was just a girl at the time.

Helen took a job in the Recorder of Deeds office, and Frederick got to know her better. A graduate of Mount Holyoke Female Seminary, Helen was an excellent writer and speaker and a suffragette. During the Civil War, she taught newly freed slaves and was a fearless journalist. Frederick was impressed with her. Despite Helen's being nineteen years younger than he was, the two fell in love.

Frederick married Helen in a secret ceremony on January 24, 1884. The next day newspapers announced their marriage with headlines such as "The Venerable Colored Orator Takes a White Wife!" The public—both black and white—were shocked. In U.S. history there had never been such a high-profile interracial marriage, and everyone had an opinion about it. Most were critical. Frederick and Helen had expected this. Frederick's vision for the United States had always been radical. He wanted it to be a country where all human beings—no matter the color of their skin—would have the right to dignity and the ability to make their own choices in life without worrying about race. He happened to have fallen in love with and chosen to marry a white woman, and he was happy to leave it at that. For her part, forty-six-year-old Helen told reporters, "Love came to me, and I was not afraid to marry the man I loved because of his color."

Frederick and Helen's marriage divided their families and friends. It seemed a bridge too far for most to accept. Even Helen's father, who had welcomed Frederick as an honored guest in his home, disinherited Helen, and Helen's mother and sisters refused to speak to her. Frederick's children felt betrayed and could not accept a white stepmother.

Eighteen months after their marriage, Frederick retired as the Recorder of Deeds for the District of Columbia, and soon after the two set off on a European tour. They crossed the Atlantic Ocean by steamer in September 1886. Great Britain was their first stop, where Frederick eagerly introduced his new wife to old friends and supporters, Ellen Richardson among them. Ellen had raised the money to buy Frederick's freedom forty years before. Because some of Frederick's other friends were long dead, he and Helen visited their graves where Frederick explained the impact these friends had made on his life. After traveling through England and Ireland, the couple moved on to France, Italy, Egypt, and Greece, taking in the pyramids, the sparkling blue water surrounding the Greek Isles, and the ancient ruins of Rome.

Frederick and Helen were away for eleven months, returning to Cedar Hill in August 1887. Although many people condemned his marriage to Helen, Frederick was a contented man. The two enjoyed each other's company, talking, reading, and learning together.

Three months after arriving back from Europe, the northern United States was ravaged by a typhoid epidemic. It ripped through the Douglass family, killing five of Frederick's grandchildren within a two-week period. Frederick was devastated but also grateful that Anna had been spared such grief.

in February 1888, Frederick turned seventy, and everyone expected his retirement to be permanent. He continued to write articles and develop new lectures for the public based upon his overseas trip. Yet he still felt that he had more to offer. In spring 1889, President Benjamin Harrison appointed him to the position of United States Minister Resident and Consul General in Haiti. Over the years Frederick had followed Haiti's highs and lows, writing in his newspapers about its relationship with the United States. Haiti was a country of firsts. It was located on the first island Christopher Columbus reached in the Caribbean, and in 1804 it became the world's first black republic. Haiti had also been the richest colony in the Caribbean, its wealth built upon a constant supply of young black men from Africa who were worked to death in the sugarcane fields and coffee plantations.

Despite also having rebelled to win their freedom and establish a republic, the United States refused to recognize Haiti. Congress had been controlled by Southern slave states who did not want to acknowledge a black republic lest it serve as an example of how previously enslaved black people could rise up and govern themselves. It wasn't until 1862, after Southern states had seceded from the Union, that the United States recognized Haiti.

On October 12, 1889, Frederick and Helen Douglass departed for Port-au-Prince aboard USS *Kearsarge,* but not without controversy. Several naval officers on the ship refused to sail with Frederick and Helen aboard, protesting their mixed-race marriage. And three days before their departure, a political upheaval took place in Haiti as Florvil Hyppolite led an uprising against President François

Légitime. Two days after the *Kearsarge* steamed into the harbor at Port-au-Prince to deliver Frederick Douglass, the newest and highest-ranking United States diplomat in the country, Hyppolite was sworn into office as Haiti's new president.

Frederick and Helen rented a grand house with tropical gardens on the hillside overlooking Port-au-Prince Bay. They were both enthralled by the beauty of the place with an abundance of brightly colored bougainvillea, thickly wooded hillside, and sparkling bay below. It reminded Frederick of the bay in Naples, Italy.

By the end of his first year in Haiti, Frederick was exhausted and angry. While the United States government had given him the title of Minister Resident and Consul General to Haiti, it had not given him the authority to do what he thought was in the best interests of the United States. That title was given to Rear Admiral Bancroft Gherardi, who had been sent by President Harrison to show the naval might of the United States and demand that Haiti give them Mole Saint-Nicholas, a deep harbor on the country's northwest coast, where the United States wanted to establish a coaling station to refuel its naval ships. This would also allow the United States to control the shipping lane between Haiti and Cuba, especially since France was trying to build a canal across the isthmus of Panama to connect the Atlantic and Pacific Oceans.

On July 30, 1891, after much wrangling, Haiti's president Hyppolite rejected the United States' demand to be allowed to establish a naval station at

Mole Saint-Nicholas. Frederick understood why. Haitians were proud of their country and did not want a foreign power annexing any of it. And although Frederick vehemently disagreed with the way Rear Admiral Gherardi had gone about the negotiations, he was the one blamed for the failure. Given this, Frederick felt he had no choice but to resign his position over his disgust at the way the U.S. State Department and American business interests had tried to maneuver and bully to acquire Mole Saint-Nicholas.

Upon returning to the United States, many people were interested in what seventy-three-year-old Frederick would do next. Would he retire or seek another position? Frederick told a newspaper reporter, "I have labored many years for the advancement of the colored race, and I shall again take up the work. I can talk and I can write. I shall use both of these methods of usefulness until I am summoned hence."

That is just what Frederick did. In spring 1892, he departed on a speaking tour through New York, Massachusetts, and New Jersey. He traveled south by train, stopping to speak at Knoxville and Nashville, Tennessee, and Atlanta, Georgia. He then traveled to Tuskegee, Alabama, where he met another well-known black leader, Booker T. Washington, and delivered Tuskegee Institute's tenth commencement address. Over five thousand people crowded the campus to hear Frederick deliver a speech that looked forward to a time when everyone would have the opportunity to live up to his or her individual potential.

Four days later, Frederick was in Rochester, New York, where he participated with President Benjamin

Harrison in the dedication of the Soldiers' and Sailors' Monument. The monument commemorated the sacrifice and effort of members of the infantry, cavalry, marines, and artillery during the Civil War. For Frederick, being back in Rochester was a day for memories.

As spring turned to summer, the Haitian government asked Frederick to be commissioner of its pavilion at the World's Columbian Exposition in Chicago the following year. Frederick made his way to Chicago to work on setting up the pavilion, and while there he met Ida B. Wells. He'd never encountered anyone quite like her. Born into slavery in Mississippi at the height of the Civil War, Ida was orphaned at sixteen. She moved to Memphis, Tennessee, and became a newspaper editor and schoolteacher. Ida told Frederick that the year before she had been fired from her teaching job because she wrote articles criticizing the Memphis Board of Education over conditions in separate colored schools. Soon afterward, three of her friends—part owners in a grocery store serving the black community—were attacked and arrested. They were then dragged from the jail by a mob of white men and hanged. Frederick remembered reading about the People's Grocery lynching. Ida explained that she was incensed by the lack of justice the three owners received. She now vowed to investigate and report on every lynching across the South. It was a dangerous undertaking, but one that Frederick could see five-foot-tall Ida intended to carry out. In her effort to expose and document what was happening to black people in the South under black codes as a lone, black women, Ida crisscrossed the South asking questions, recording statements, reading local accounts, and witnessing white mobs in action.

Meeting Ida Wells put a new spring in Frederick's step. He recognized the glint of steely determination in her eyes. He'd seen it before in the eyes of his old abolitionist friends. He was sure that Ida would continue to be on the forefront of the next generation, calling the people of the United States to live up to their high constitutional ideals.

Frederick returned from planning the pavilion in Chicago, after which tragedy struck his family once more. This time his namesake son, Frederick Jr., died of tuberculosis at the age of fifty. It was a hard blow to bear as Frederick watched his son's body lowered into the grave beside his son's wife, Virginia, who had died of a hemorrhage when Frederick was in Haiti. This had left Frederick Jr. with ten-year-old Charles and three-year-old Robert to care for. One of Rosetta's daughters would now watch over Frederick Jr.'s two orphaned sons.

Much of the following year was taken up with planning and overseeing the Haitian pavilion at the World's Columbian Exposition in Chicago. During this time, Frederick was able to spend more time with Ida Wells, who by now had compiled a long list of lynchings throughout the South. Because Frederick wanted to lend his voice to her research, he worked hard on a new lecture. "Lessons of the Hour" was a powerful call to audiences everywhere that the United States was a country of laws and that those laws must apply to *all* people in *all* places at *all* times. Anything less mocked the Constitution and turned the country into a land where no one was truly safe.

Delivering this message in Baltimore in 1894, Frederick concluded his speech with, "I hope and trust all will come out right in the end, but the immediate future looks dark and troubled. I cannot shut my eyes to the ugly facts before me."

On the morning of February 20, 1895, Frederick and Helen took a carriage into Washington, D.C. Helen was dropped off at the Library of Congress to do some research. Frederick continued on to Metzerott Hall on F Street for a meeting of the National Women's Council. As he walked in, Frederick received a standing ovation from the crowd. Susan B. Anthony beckoned him to sit with her on stage. Frederick beamed. He'd always been and still was a proud supporter of women's right to vote.

At seven o'clock that evening, a carriage pulled up at Cedar Hill to take Frederick to a local black church where he was scheduled to speak. Standing at the bottom of the stairs, Frederick suddenly grasped at his chest and collapsed. Helen ran outside and shouted for the carriage driver to get help. But it was too late. Frederick Douglass had died of a heart attack.

Five days later, Helen Douglass, Frederick's three surviving children, Rosetta, Lewis, and Charles, and his grandchildren gathered at Cedar Hill. They held a private funeral service in the parlor before accompanying Frederick's embalmed body on one last public tour. The first stop for his casket and its entourage was a funeral service at his home church, the Metropolitan AME Church in Washington, D.C. As expected, this was a well-attended event. Everyone from congressmen to farmworkers were in attendance to pay their respects. The service lasted four hours, after which the casket was escorted by 150 black Grand Army of the Republic soldiers to the train station. The next stop was New York City, where Frederick lay in state at City Hall. Thousands of New Yorkers filed by for one last glimpse of the man who had arrived at their shore as an escaped slave fifty-seven years earlier. Frederick's casket was then loaded aboard a train bound for Rochester, New York. The city had closed its schools and draped City Hall in black bunting—loosely woven cloth—as a show of respect. Frederick Douglass, the man whom the city claimed as one of their own, had returned to be buried there.

It was a fitting farewell. Frederick was a man who had stood tall and dignified as a spokesperson for three generations of black people: those enslaved before the Civil War, those disoriented after being emancipated, and those experiencing the oppression of black codes and the threat of lynching. He had served them all with his voice and his pen. His words would remain an echo for generations to come.

"What I ask for the negro is not benevolence, not pity, not sympathy, but simply justice." —Frederick Douglass

Bibliography

Blight, David W. *Frederick Douglass: Prophet of Freedom.* New York: Simon & Schuster Paperbacks, 2018.

Bingham, Caleb. *The Columbian Orator (Bicentennial Edition).* New York University Press, 1998.

Douglass, Frederick. *The Complete Autobiographies of Frederick Douglass.* Radford, VA: Wilder Publications, LLC., 2008.

Katz, William Loren. *Breaking the Chains: African-American Slave Resistance.* New York: Atheneum, 1990.

Preston, Dickson J. *Young Frederick Douglass: The Maryland Years.* New York: Johns Hopkins University Press, 2018.

John Stauffer, Zoe Trodd, and Celeste-Marie Bernier. *Picturing Frederick Douglass: An Illustrated Biography of the Nineteenth Century's Most Photographed American.* New York: Liveright Publishing Corporation, 2015.

Wells, Jonathan Daniel. *The Kidnapping Club: Wall Street, Slavery, and Resistance on the Eve of the Civil War.* Bold Type Books, 2020.

About the Authors

Janet and Geoff Benge are a husband and wife writing team with more than thirty years of writing experience. Janet is a former elementary school teacher. Geoff holds a degree in history. Originally from New Zealand, the Benges spent ten years serving with Youth With A Mission. They have two daughters, Laura and Shannon, and an adopted son, Lito. They make their home in the Orlando, Florida, area.

Also from Janet and Geoff Benge...

More adventure-filled biographies for ages 10 to 100!

Gladys Aylward: The Adventure of a Lifetime • 978-1-57658-019-6
Nate Saint: On a Wing and a Prayer • 978-1-57658-017-2
Hudson Taylor: Deep in the Heart of China • 978-1-57658-016-5
Amy Carmichael: Rescuer of Precious Gems • 978-1-57658-018-9
Eric Liddell: Something Greater Than Gold • 978-1-57658-137-7
Corrie ten Boom: Keeper of the Angels' Den • 978-1-57658-136-0
William Carey: Obliged to Go • 978-1-57658-147-6
George Müller: Guardian of Bristol's Orphans • 978-1-57658-145-2
Jim Elliot: One Great Purpose • 978-1-57658-146-9
Mary Slessor: Forward into Calabar • 978-1-57658-148-3
David Livingstone: Africa's Trailblazer • 978-1-57658-153-7
Betty Greene: Wings to Serve • 978-1-57658-152-0
Adoniram Judson: Bound for Burma • 978-1-57658-161-2
Cameron Townsend: Good News in Every Language • 978-1-57658-164-3
Jonathan Goforth: An Open Door in China • 978-1-57658-174-2
Lottie Moon: Giving Her All for China • 978-1-57658-188-9
John Williams: Messenger of Peace • 978-1-57658-256-5
William Booth: Soup, Soap, and Salvation • 978-1-57658-258-9
Rowland Bingham: Into Africa's Interior • 978-1-57658-282-4
Ida Scudder: Healing Bodies, Touching Hearts • 978-1-57658-285-5
Wilfred Grenfell: Fisher of Men • 978-1-57658-292-3
Lillian Trasher: The Greatest Wonder in Egypt • 978-1-57658-305-0
Loren Cunningham: Into All the World • 978-1-57658-199-5
Florence Young: Mission Accomplished • 978-1-57658-313-5
Sundar Singh: Footprints Over the Mountains • 978-1-57658-318-0
C.T. Studd: No Retreat • 978-1-57658-288-6
Rachel Saint: A Star in the Jungle • 978-1-57658-337-1
Brother Andrew: God's Secret Agent • 978-1-57658-355-5
Clarence Jones: Mr. Radio • 978-1-57658-343-2
Count Zinzendorf: Firstfruit • 978-1-57658-262-6
John Wesley: The World His Parish • 978-1-57658-382-1
C. S. Lewis: Master Storyteller • 978-1-57658-385-2
David Bussau: Facing the World Head-on • 978-1-57658-415-6
Jacob DeShazer: Forgive Your Enemies • 978-1-57658-475-0

Isobel Kuhn: On the Roof of the World • 978-1-57658-497-2
Elisabeth Elliot: Joyful Surrender • 978-1-57658-513-9
D. L. Moody: Bringing Souls to Christ • 978-1-57658-552-8
Paul Brand: Helping Hands • 978-1-57658-536-8
Dietrich Bonhoeffer: In the Midst of Wickedness • 978-1-57658-713-3
Francis Asbury: Circuit Rider • 978-1-57658-737-9
Samuel Zwemer: The Burden of Arabia • 978-1-57658-738-6
Klaus-Dieter John: Hope in the Land of the Incas • 978-1-57658-826-2
Mildred Cable: Through the Jade Gate • 978-1-57658-886-4
John Flynn: Into the Never Never • 978-1-57658-898-7
Richard Wurmbrand: Love Your Enemies • 978-1-57658-987-8
Charles Mulli: We Are Family • 978-1-57658-894-9
John Newton: Change of Heart • 978-1-57658-909-0
Helen Roseveare: Mama Luka • 978-1-57658-910-6
Norman Grubb: Mission Builder • 978-1-57658-915-1
Albert Schweitzer: Le Grand Docteur • 978-1-57658-961-8
Frederick Douglass: The Right to dignity • 978-1-62486-151-2

Available in paperback, e-book, and audiobook formats.

HEROES OF HISTORY are available in paperback, e-book, and audiobook formats, with more titles coming soon! Curriculum Guides are also available for all U.S. biographies.

www.Heroesofhistory.com